ADDISON MIZNER

ADDISON MIZNER

A Palm Beach Memoir

The Historical Society of Palm Beach County

Original Memoir by Addison Mizner

Introduction by Alice DeLamar

Edited by Augustus Mayhew III

Pineapple Press

Palm Beach, Florida

An imprint of Globe Pequot, the trade division of
The Rowman & Littlefield Publishing Group, Inc.
4501 Forbes Blvd., Ste. 200
Lanham, MD 20706
www.rowman.com

Distributed by NATIONAL BOOK NETWORK

British Library Cataloguing in Publication Information available

Library of Congress Cataloging-in-Publication Data available

ISBN 978-1-68334-360-8 (HC : alk. paper)
ISBN 978-1-68334-361-5 (electronic)

∞™ The paper used in this publication meets the minimum requirements of American National Standard for Information Sciences—Permanence of Paper for Printed Library Materials, ANSI/NISO Z39.48-1992.

For Paris Singer

I think posterity should know what great vision he had, and that Palm Beach would still be a dirty old sand spit if it had not been for him.

Addison Mizner, July 14, 1932
Letter to Joan Bates Singer on the death of Paris Singer

Addison Mizner (1872–1933).

CONTENTS

EDITOR'S NOTE

Addison Mizner died while he was working on his memoir's second volume that would include thoughts and recollections about his Palm Beach years. Mizner was only able to put together the events from 1918 until 1924 with his secretary, who transcribed them into a typed manuscript.

For clarity and smoothness, the original text's stream-of-consciousness sentence structure and narrative sequence were attuned to better express Mizner's intent. Idiosyncratic jargon remains, adding nuance to Mizner's unfiltered character and outspoken opinions. Endnotes inform the reader's familiarity with Mizner's family and friends. Addison Mizner and Alice DeLamar's views and observations stand as they were expressed, reflecting their knowledge at the time.

Unless otherwise noted, all images are from the Historical Society of Palm Beach County's Addison Mizner Collection.

ACKNOWLEDGMENTS

Since 1937 the Historical Society of Palm Beach County has collected, preserved, and exhibited the documents and artifacts recording the people and events that have shaped the area's cultural, social, and political history. The Historical Society's archive details Palm Beach County's development with more than four million photographs, vintage maps, pioneer histories, and the area's largest collection of architectural drawings.

"My houses are full of history," said Addison Mizner.[1] Fortunately, for residents and researchers alike, the Historical Society of Palm Beach County has long recognized the important role Addison Mizner played in the history of Palm Beach County, having organized and maintained the extensive Addison Mizner Collection.

The Mizner archive is composed of the architect's extensive portfolio of drawings and photographs of his Palm Beach mansions and buildings, as well as drawings from earlier commissions, his unfinished Boca Raton project, and his final works. The collection also includes his business records documenting the expansion and impact of Mizner Industries. These significant research materials are enhanced with exemplars of Mizner's creations—floor and roof tiles, pottery, cast stones, and furnishings that found their way into many of the area's houses built during the 1920s. The Historical Society's chief curator, Debi Murray, and research director, Rose Guerrero, maintain and manage the collection, making it accessible to researchers, architects, historians, and owners of Mizner-designed properties.

The Historical Society acquired Addison Mizner's unpublished manuscript as a result of the foresight and discernment of Alice DeLamar, a patron of Mizner's, and the perseverance of E. Harris Drew, Mizner's lawyer and estate executor. In April 1958, Ysabel Chase Hollins, Mizner's principal heir, instructed Drew to dispose of her uncle's unpublished manuscript, leaving the matter to his judgment. Having moved from Palm Beach to become a justice of the Florida Supreme Court in Tallahassee, Drew worked with DeLamar to determine the most suitable repository. They decided to donate it to the Historical Society of Palm Beach County, then housed at Whitehall with the Flagler Museum.

DeLamar accompanied the manuscript with letters detailing her friendship and admiration for Mizner as well as her impressions of the people, places, and circumstances surrounding their shared early years at Palm Beach. Her lifetime support for Mizner's work was as impassioned as her patronage for social causes and artists. When DeLamar's determined efforts and philanthropic largesse resulted in the seminal publication of *The Florida Architecture of Addison Mizner* in 1927, Mizner inscribed a copy for Alice with, "To Alice. My Lorenzo the Magnificent, Addison."

FOREWORD

Since the publication of Addison Mizner's autobiographical chronicle *The Many Mizners* in 1932, there has been little attention, except for the occasional quip, on the architect's personal observations and perspectives, whereas his houses and buildings have been the subject of numerous books.

That earlier volume told of the Mizner family's standing in Northern California's history and recounted his adventuresome early years before resettling in New York and coming to Palm Beach. Mizner's travels had taken him to far-flung places where he met the most extraordinary people. After *The Many*

The Mizner family in Benicia, California. Addison was the seventh of eight siblings. Back row: Edgar. Second row: Ella, Lansing Jr., William. Third row: Lansing Sr., Wilson, Mary Ysabel (Minnie), Henry. Front row, left: Addison. LIBRARY OF CONGRESS

Mizners met with a favorable response, the *Palm Beach Post* book reviewer wrote in 1932, "The second volume on which Mizner is at work will be waited even more eagerly by Palm Beach, for it is with his life here that it will deal." After all, Palm Beach would make for the most productive years of the architect's life and where he found his place in history.

Hence, this companion chronicle begins with Mizner finding his way to Palm Beach after a serendipitous meeting with philanthropist and sewing-machine heir Paris Singer. While Mizner was recovering from a leg injury in New York, a mutual friend introduced them, and their shared interests made for an immediate friendship.

After hearing Mizner's account of Guatemala's architectural and cultural heritage, Singer organized an expedition for them to spend the following winter there. But when Guatemala was devastated by a major earthquake, he invited Mizner to his Palm Beach cottage, where the warm weather would aid his recovery.

Mizner shares with readers the story of how he and Paris Singer came to Palm Beach and transformed one of Henry Flagler's hotel whistle-stops into an international resort. The narrative ends in 1924 with Mizner at the height of his architectural success, only months before pursuing his Boca Raton development that brought about his financial collapse.

As a result of the opportunities Paris Singer had afforded him, Mizner was able to expand his talents, achieving national recognition and financial success. At Palm Beach, he juggled the daily pressures from his own architectural projects with the added demands from his varied development and manufacturing interests that called on him to meet the exhaustive requirements of other architects and builders. Regrettably, he would never slow down enough to fully overcome his chronic heart condition. Addison Mizner died in February 1933, only a few months after his memoir was published but before he completed the follow-up narrative.

Now, ninety years after Mizner completed the first volume of his memoirs, the Historical Society of Palm Beach County's publication of his incomplete manuscript recounts in Mizner's own words his Palm Beach achievements within the context of his interactions with family, friends, and coworkers. The Historical Society's volume offers readers Mizner's unvarnished perspective on his remarkable accomplishments and the larger-than-life characters who gave Palm Beach its incomparable allure.

With a mix of Barbary Coast bluster and Noel Coward drawing-room wit, Mizner brings to light the people who worked for him, the clients he assisted, and most important, his family relationships, especially with his younger brother, Wilson; his nephew, Horace; and his niece, Ysabel Chase Hollins. His *carpe diem* sensibility allowed him to put aside setbacks and brush aside disappointments. Mizner's account of a madcap dinner party, where one of his guests had passed out in a limousine and was carried into his house, makes for an unforgettable Palm Beach moment.

In addition to the donation of Mizner's memoir to the Historical Society, arts patron and mining heiress Alice DeLamar's introduction shares her insights about Mizner and her close friendships with his family. Readers will appreciate hearing their voices with the same clarity as if they might have been overheard on Worth Avenue coming from Mizner's terrace while he was hosting one of his Sunday afternoon musicales. This untold story of Addison Mizner and Alice DeLamar at Palm Beach makes for a unique historical viewpoint.

Alice DeLamar first visited Palm Beach following her debutante ball in 1915. A student at Manhattan's Miss Spence's School, she lived with her wealthy father, Joseph DeLamar, in an East Side Manhattan townhouse and at Pembroke, a Long Island estate set on forty-six acres with an eighty-two-room, sixty-thousand-square-foot mansion. Following the death of her father in 1918, Alice inherited a $10-million trust fund and ownership of Pembroke.[1]

A member of the Palm Beach Women's Aviation Association and the Everglades Club's Ladies Auxiliary, Alice was introduced to Mizner by his nephew Horace Chase Jr. in January 1920. At the time, Mizner and Chase were living at El Solano, the first house Mizner had designed for himself, located at 720 South Ocean Boulevard. Horace and Alice shared a love of aviation. She and pharmaceutical heiress Evangeline Johnson made national headlines when they flew over The Breakers, dropping hundreds of flyers protesting the hotel's beach censor who regulated women's bathing attire. DeLamar and Mizner's lives intertwined socially, and according to DeLamar, immediately became like family.

Addison and Alice were out-of-the-ordinary personalities who found refuge at Palm Beach, where their private and public lives reflected the era's laissez-faire ambiance. Their story recalls a more informal Palm Beach when Wall Street millionaires were as at ease attending a black-tie dinner dance in a hotel ballroom as having lunch with their carpenters and gardeners. Mizner's patrons, DeLamar among them, were among the nation's wealthiest and most discerning clientele who expected no less than the best. They valued Mizner's up-at-dawn work ethic and his leisurely charismatic sociability, whether at an Animal Rescue League meeting or a fancy-dress ball at the Everglades Club.

Mizner's constantly moving vignettes display his tireless patience, whether dealing with Eva Stotesbury's indecision as to her private bathroom's location or coping with Paris Singer's volatile personality. Mizner recalls, "What fun it all was, showing men how to stucco, teaching others how to cure pip in chickens, clearing jungles, killing land crabs with gas, catching new alligators in the Everglades, and planning ahead for every little detail to be ready to slip into place."

His summer European buying trip with client Eleanor "Nell" Cosden and her assistant, Peggy Thayer, made for a memorable odyssey in 1923, leaving him to write, "We laughed our way through the happiest two months of my life. When they dumped me off on a street corner in Nice, tears were standing in my eyes."

At the time, Mizner's signature resort style was touted by the nation's leading architectural journals. Architectural historian Matlack Price proclaimed the Gulf Stream Golf Club "one of the most attractive Spanish-Italian adaptations in the United States. It has decided charm."[2] The Palm Beach Company began building Phipps Plaza with several Mizner-designed storefronts. In May 1924, the *Palm Beach Post* termed Mizner's architectural and manufacturing business "the largest resort business in this part of the world."

Although public praise bolstered Mizner's confidence, he valued his private interactions with family and friends. On the evening of December 12, 1924, Bill and Lucy Kingsley arranged a surprise birthday party for Addison at Via Mizner. As the festivities went late into the night, Jay O'Brien read a birthday poem he had written on Renaissance-style illuminated parchment. The poem began with "You have painted us a city, your pigments stone and tile" and ended with "There is nothing more to reach, your biography, just beauty. And your monument—Palm Beach."[3]

That same year, during the week after Christmas, Mizner opened the door of his apartment to find the head of the painter's union joined by a delegation of members. The painter's national union had issued a proclamation inducting Addison Mizner as an honorary member of their organization. He was honored for the "inspiration he has given to the Palm Beaches for his architecture and the artistry in which he has handled the interior and exterior painting of the marvelous buildings he has designed and executed here." Mizner was overwhelmed by the honor, "the only gentleman in the South to enjoy this privilege."

Several months later, just as Paris Singer had gone north of Palm Beach to develop his next venture, Mizner announced plans to build "the world's most architecturally beautiful playground" thirty miles south of Palm Beach. His Mizner Development Company had acquired sixteen hundred acres and two miles of oceanfront in Boca Raton. The days and weeks to come would challenge Mizner's resilient spirit, his wit, and his wisdom.

Addison Mizner, Marie Calhoun, with Joan and Paris Singer, Palm Beach.

Just a week after Mizner's death, a local newspaper reported that Mizner was unable to finish his memoir's second volume, and its disposition remained unknown. "The Book Nook mourns that it will never be available to the public. For in it, Addison Mizner told his own inside story of Palm Beach, told it with his own irresistible wit, with his blind disregard for the crime of *lese majeste* . . . The fact that it was left unfinished and unpublished is regretted."[4]

Although almost a century has passed since the Sears Publishing Company promised Mizner's society tell-all would be in bookstores for the 1933 season, this memoir takes twenty-first-century readers inside the heart and mind of a Palm Beach original—an architectural genius whose family and friends were as important to him as the iconic legacy of the houses and buildings he designed.

Augustus Mayhew III

Portrait of Alice DeLamar, artist unknown.

Alice DeLamar
Remembering Addison

The second part of Addison Mizner's autobiography was, of course, unfinished, as he died before he could get it into shape. He dictated the chapters to his secretary when he was a very sick man. He had no ghostwriter. Mizner was never a professional writer, though he was the most amusing and charming of raconteurs. He had a great way with an anecdote and a constant unfailing wit. When Addison died, his lawyer, E. Harris Drew, settled his estate. But Drew never had a copy of Mizner's manuscript made to send to his niece Ysabel Chase Hollins, who took care of him at the end. Ysabel never saw it.

In the days when Ysabel was in Palm Beach, spending many winters with her uncle Addison, he had moved to his Worth Avenue tower house and had plenty of guest space. Ysabel was drinking just about what the other people drank, and there the problem of alcoholism was not in sight at that time. There also must have been plenty of money in that Hollins family, and I don't know where it all went. But one heard only the worst reports that filtered back from California.

The handsome Pebble Beach house that Addison designed and built for Ysabel must have been sold off when her son, Kim Hollins, was still very young.[1] It was probably when Kim was about fourteen that Harris Drew first heard about his being troubled. With Drew's help, it was arranged to send him to a boarding school, where he stayed until he joined the navy at about the age of seventeen. I never heard any further report from this direction. I remember how Addison used to carry a photo of that baby in his wallet. He showed it around proudly to everyone and would then say, "Don't you think he looks like me?" Of course, most babies do resemble their plump balding relatives; as Mr. Churchill used to say quite rightly, "but all babies look like me."

Addison took a very dim view of excessive drinking. In his own house, at least, he wanted everything kept at a dignified level. He hated to go out. It was hardly more than once a year, in his later years, that he could be persuaded to get dressed up and appear at some event at the Everglades Club, usually the New Year's opening.

He liked to receive his friends in his big living room in the afternoon for cocktails. The butler served them in small antique silver cups, unless you asked for something different. A Jamaica rum cocktail was the specialty of the house. You got served one, or possibly two, but not a third, and you did not help yourself at the bar. He often gave informal dinner parties during the winter season. There you were served wine. After dinner, the butler would bring one or perhaps two highballs, but not a third, and you did not help yourself to whiskey either.

Before the year that Wilson, Addison's brother, brought Florence back to Palm Beach and introduced her around as Mrs. Wilson Mizner, he had lived at Addison's house.[2] But after the bride had arrived in the middle 1920s, Addison built for Wilson a house of his own on Worth Avenue, a duplex house with a wide front-yard garden. He could derive rent from the ground-floor apartment while he and Florence occupied the upper floor. The ground floor of this place has now been incorporated into a coffee shop and several boutiques. The shops have covered

Wilson Mizner residence, 237 Worth Avenue.

what was once the yard, so nothing of it is now recognizable. The upstairs apartment, with its balcony and large studio living room, is still rented out and occupied each year. When I was house building here myself, I was often down here in midsummer.

I have a recollection of walking down Worth Avenue one day around noon, seeing Wilson out on his balcony leaning on the rail and smoking a cigar with several days' growth of beard on his face and wearing an old-fashioned nightshirt. He was a truly comic sight that day. Speaking of shirts, I can't imagine where the legend came from that tells of Addison originating the fashion of wearing sport shirts on the outside. No one ever saw Addison in any shirt that was not tucked in. The fashion obviously came from Manila to Hawaii, to California, and then to Florida.

When Horace Chase, the nephew, first came down here, he stayed at Addison's house for a while.[3] Later, he moved to a shack he constructed with timbers and palm thatch. Then, he built a larger house near the inlet after he made an astonishing sum of money almost by accident. He had bought, for a small down payment, a piece of an island with a lovely beach adjoining Nassau, where a first-class tourist hotel did not yet exist. Within a year, the boom was on in Nassau, too. The British Colonial Hotel was built, and the hotel company, which was owned by the Munson shipping line, paid Horace $100,000 for his beach and a piece of the island. During the boom days such jackpots were not too unusual. This was Paradise Beach, of course.

When Horace first came to Palm Beach, he had just left the Canadian Flying Corps. He hitchhiked to Florida to see if his uncle could find him a job. He was then about nineteen. He had lied about his age when he joined up but had stayed long enough to learn to fly and to become middleweight boxing champion of the Canadian flyers.

El Solano, aerial. 720 South Ocean Boulevard. Addison Mizner's first Palm Beach residence that he designed for himself, naming it for Solano County, California, where he was raised.

The house that Addison lived in then was small but very charming. It was the first one that he built here for himself.[4] He settled in with no idea that someone would soon come along and offer him so large a price for his place that he could not afford not to sell. It had a delightful interior; the living room was lined with books and paneled in local cypress wood. This cypress wood called pecky had only been used for scaffold and cement forms before Addison's day. He discovered the decorative possibilities of its texture and used it widely. The house faced the beach and had a thick growth of jungle trees behind it, where he had cleared space for a small patio with a tiled fountain. The patio was always a lively spot with several pet raccoons, chow puppies, a pet monkey, and a large macaw parrot. Addison always had to have a veritable zoo around him to be happy.

El Solano, library-study.

A founding member of Palm Beach's Animal Rescue League, Addison Mizner cared for a menagerie of household pets.

That first summer of 1919, when Horace was at Addison's house, he was out in the sea one day and got badly bitten on the leg by a barracuda. Fortunately, one of the young draftsmen who worked for Addison was also present and helped him get out of the water and carried him to the house. A doctor was called. He said that the leg must be amputated at the knee. Horace indignantly said, "You'll cut off my neck first!"

So, the doctor gave it a chance and sewed up all the gashes without any anesthetic. Horace hobbled about on crutches for six or eight months and eventually made a complete recovery, and then he could jump over a hurdle better than most. When I first met him, he was on crutches. It was Horace who first took me to his uncle's house. Horace inherited the quick Mizner wit. He also might have made a good architect if he had studied or been trained. He had a certain inborn taste and a sense of good proportions.

Building work intrigued him, and he caught on right away. He had an instinct for it. He never became a professional at it. Yet, he got actual orders to build three or four small houses for friends of his, carrying out these jobs with very attractive results.[5] His own house near the inlet was built with only local labor and himself, working with them and supervising. They practically made it up as they went along. Horace was much less capable of drawing a floor plan than I was.

Needless to say, in those days such a thing as a building code did not exist, and you could construct about anything you pleased. All along the coast, there were groups of squatters in thatched huts when the boom began attracting people to the South. I had watched Addison often making beautiful watercolor sketches of his building jobs. I saw these turned over to the various young draftsmen who worked for him, along with rough plans worked out on squared paper, photos of details of doorways and balconies, and other items from authentic Spanish houses to be drawn up into a working blueprint.

I soon caught on to the procedures of building, too, and after a very thorough search for what I decided was the most desirable piece of land I could find, I also started to build something very small that was later added to and enlarged. As this was in 1922, I had plenty of choice plots of land to choose from. The boom was in its very early period. Addison was pleased at Horace's knack for building, as he saw his efforts taking shape. He was amused at my attempting building, too, and thought that I was also getting quite a nice result. There was never any architect involved at my place, only an engineer-building contractor.[6]

Of course, I had the benefit of all the skilled artisans that Mizner Industries attracted to this region—skilled masons, tile setters, metalworkers, and carpenters, who were often practically cabinetmakers, such was their skill. There was quality available in those days that you just can't find anymore. Every other architect working down here at the time used Mizner Industries products. Marion Wyeth, Howard Major, Maurice Fatio, all of them people of talent, used Mizner's Spanish-style roof and floor tiles, both terra-cotta, handmade right here in West Palm Beach, wrought-iron forges, and the cabinetmakers of the furniture works. All the other architects made use of these people Mizner had imported and set up in workshops. The more work the industries got, the better. They did not work for Mizner exclusively as some may have supposed.

After Horace built his own house, he counted on having it for himself and for his group of friends, but it did not turn out that way. As soon as Papa Chase,[7] in California, heard that his son was building a house, he decided to pack up and come live with him. Horace had not counted on that at all, and it rather took the wind out of his sails. Pop Chase was an Edwardian gentleman who wore a velvet smoking jacket to dinner every evening, who played tennis with enthusiasm, and who dearly loved his whiskey. Pop Chase arrived shortly before the house near the inlet was completed.

During the housebuilding, wanting to be near the job, Horace rented an old houseboat moored on the lake, a former

Mizner Industries, Bunker Road, West Palm Beach. Craftsmen and sales staff photographed with an array of cast stone products.

floating restaurant that was rather rundown and lacking repair. Not only was Pop there, but Ysabel as well, as Addison was away in Spain buying furniture, and his house was closed. There was also a cook named Sam and an Airedale dog.

One morning very early Sam woke up, smelled smoke, and went back to sleep. Then Pop woke up, smelled smoke, and went back to sleep, and so did Ysabel. Then Horace woke up, smelled smoke, leaped out, and got the inmates and the dog off the boat just before it went up in flames from a short circuit. No insurance, of course. All the clothes and equipment were gone. There was no choice but to camp out in the uncompleted house, but they managed. That was typically the Chase family!

Wilson, since his own house was not yet built at that time, used to come down to Horace's house almost every afternoon and drink his fill. Very often Anita Loos was with him, as they were great cronies.[8] Anita drank very moderately and was always amused by Wilson. Horace liked Anita very much, but he was overly tolerant and hospitable to Wilson, who would do him a mean turn whenever he could. Horace knew it well. Wilson would find ways to get Horace in wrong with Addison however he could and was always watching for chances. He never dared to try to undermine Ysabel, however. He was afraid of her sharp tongue, and Addison was too solidly devoted to his niece to ever hear a word against her.

The family scheming was always in Wilson's mind though. Addison had the money, at the time, and if any favors were to be handed out, Wilson wanted to get them himself. He was the baby brother and had not been of any credit to the family thus far. I suppose by wishful thinking Addison still hoped to see Wilson respectable and respected if circumstances gave him the chance. If Anita Loos has as good a memory as I think she has, she ought to remember a lot of amusing things about Addison and Wilson in those years of 1924, 1925, and 1926, when she was down here every winter. She saw them all the time.

I remember a small episode typical of Wilson's troublemaking. Mrs. Stotesbury's ballroom was having some alterations done.[9] The work had to be finished by a certain date because of a party she was giving. A wrought-iron railing had to be finished, and the head blacksmith, an Italian, was busy at it. Horace dropped by at the forge at closing hour to bring an iron lantern that needed mending. The blacksmith's car battery was run down, and Horace offered to drive him home.

They stopped at Horace's thatched shack on the way (it was before the houseboat), and they had a glass of red wine. Then they stopped again to chat and had another. At this point, Wilson came by to show Horace the Cairn Terrier puppy he had just acquired. The unfortunate sequel was that after Horace took the blacksmith home, the man went off on a three-day binge. He never returned to work in time to finish Mrs. Stotesbury's ironwork job, and there was plenty of trouble about it.

Wilson lost no time in telling Addison that Horace got his blacksmith drunk and was to blame for the whole episode. This was quite untrue, but Addison believed it. He refused to even speak to Horace for several months. At once, he dismissed him from his job as manager at the tile factory and made Wilson head of the tile factory in his place. Of course, one was about as incompetent to run a factory as the other, but so it was with all the Mizner Industries. At that time, Jack Roy, an ex-jockey from Jacksonville, was head of the furniture works. It is a wonder Addison's interests went on as well as they did, what with all the incompetents that he surrounded himself with most of the time.

In the second half of this memoir, Addison gets in a lot of laughs poking fun at his patron, Paris Singer. There was often a bit of antagonism between them. In the long run, Singer was always the one to patch up their differences. He appreciated Addison's unique taste and ability, and he needed his cooperation. Singer did not quite have Addison's sense of humor, but he did have a great sense of fun at times. Singer himself was a man of great charm, taste, and culture.

One might not quite get that impression from some of Addison's descriptions of the capricious antics of Singer's courtship with his last wife, or transforming the rather dull wooden beach cottage on Peruvian Avenue into a pseudo-Chinese pavilion with an exotic paint job and stuffed alligators from the souvenir shops decorating the roof cornice. But he was enjoying some fun and nonsense to pass the time in the dull season of the year. The Everglades Club, incidentally, was built on the edge of a tract of jungle swampland, where the wheelchair bicycle pushers used to drive the tourists to visit Alligator Joe's Zoo along

Chinese villa and garden. Originally built in 1917, Paris Singer's cottage on Peruvian Avenue was later transformed into a Chinese-style villa by architect Addison Mizner.

winding paths in the days before there was any such thing as an actual motor road in Palm Beach. The jungle zoo was there long before the building boom.

The crest and emblem Singer chose for the Everglades Club was an alligator standing up. This has been somewhat modified in the club emblem of the present day. Singer was, of course, the first owner and president as well when the club first opened. He was paying Addison an annual retainer fee to stay on and work here in Palm Beach exclusively. Singer was an excellent host and saw to it that every detail at the club was as luxurious and elegant as possible.

The first time I ever remember meeting Singer was in the south of France, where he was in the process of building a large villa overlooking the sea on Cap Ferrat. He was living in the gatehouse of the property to oversee the work. He was building his own design, without any architect, and it was my impression that he was making a lot of mistakes in his proportions. It is not just any person of taste who can have the knack to be an amateur architect, and the larger the funds that are spent, the larger the mistakes can be.[10]

In the private yacht harbor below the villa, Singer had not one but two Curtis Seagull wooden flying boats. He was also learning to pilot the planes. He lived in truly royal style. He was a very tall man, perhaps six foot three. At that time, he wore a beard, which suited him exceptionally well. He looked like a Renaissance king. I thought he looked somewhat less distinguished the year following when he took off the beard, but this was at Cap Ferrat in 1919.

Around 1922, he sent for Sir Oswald Birley, the royal portrait painter, to come over from England and do a portrait of him. He even built a large villa and studio for Birley on the Club property. Singer could seldom be persuaded to sit still and pose. However, he would remain still and attentive whenever there was any good music to listen to. The portrait Birley did hangs in the entrance hall of the Everglades Club, but it is not a good likeness at all. It in no way suggests the dynamic character that he really was. This failure, however, can only be blamed on the difficulty Sir Oswald had getting him to pose. Anyone who has read Isadora Duncan's autobiography will recognize Singer (by the name of Lohengrin) in many of the chapters.

The first year the club was opened, Singer's two oldest sons, Cecil and Paris Jr., arrived here. Both of them were tall, good-looking, charming, young men, with none of their father's energy, however. Another son, who had been in business in Australia, also turned up. This one was short, plump, and dumpy. A daughter also arrived, Winnaretta, who was tall and very plain

Everglades Club, aerial with Via Mizner and Via Parigi towers in distance. Lower right, portrait artist Sir Oswald Birley's home and studio, 1925. Addison Mizner, architect.

and had little idea how to dress well. She was named after her aunt, Singer's sister. Princess Winnaretta de Polignac, famous in Paris and Venice, was a patroness of the young Isadora Duncan. Singer always seemed very bored with all his children, and I think they were all relieved to be away from him. I do not remember any of them turning up down here in other years, while he was still around.[11] I did not envy them having such a capricious egotist for a father.

He could never stand not having his own way about everything. Mizner's memoir draws a good deal of humor out of Singer's difficult character. Yet, on the other hand, no one could say that Singer could not be exceptionally charming when he chose to, and socially he was always a delightful host. His vast income got tied up in what was a bankruptcy. While liquidating debts from his failed Singer Island project, with its Blue Heron Hotel half built and abandoned, he died in a London hotel. I heard about it from one of the young Italian mural painters who did the murals at the Cosden villa and the Rea house under Mizner's direction.[12]

Paris Singer's two oldest sons came back to Palm Beach in the early thirties, after his death, because of their financial interest in the Everglades Club and its connection with the Singer estate.[13] It was the Depression years then, and the club was very nearly lost to its members. Stock in the club had been acquired by real estate speculators, and its fate was in jeopardy. It was Hugh Dillman, then married to Anna Thomson Dodge, who rallied the membership to buy back all the stock and reorganized the club's finances.

Addison was dead by that time, too.[14] His Ritz-Carlton Cloister Hotel at Boca Raton, where Marie Dressler[15] had been hostess, and which caused him all his financial difficulties, had already changed hands several times. It had been so transformed that the beautiful original building was no longer recognizable at all. Addison never built a house for Singer, though he had an elaborate apartment on the upper floors of the club. Singer used to say, "Each house that Addison builds is more beautiful than the one before. Thus, I shall hope to live in the last of the houses that Addison builds which will be the most beautiful of all." The actuality became quite otherwise. There was a point of diminishing returns.

After Boca Raton, Addison's health failed rapidly. He was no longer able to give the individual attention to every detail of his building jobs. His heart was giving him trouble. At Johns Hopkins, they said he must lose some weight. Doctors managed to get about forty pounds off him at one time. He said that instead of feeling better he felt much worse, so he put the pounds back on again. Though he drank very little, he was always a heavy eater. His meals were always served on silver plates that his father had brought from Guatemala. His own plate was larger than the others. I bought it at the auction that was held at his Worth Avenue apartment, and I have it in New York.

The orders for houses continued to mount in his office and were turned out largely by his staff for several years. The work had the familiar characteristics of Mizner houses. The Spanish-type roof tiles and floor tiles were still made at Mizner Industries in West Palm Beach, but they did not have the artistry, the element of picturesque, and the inimitable Mizner touch. Finally, his office could no longer accept any orders whatsoever, and people realized how seriously ill he was. Mizner Industries continued turning out their tiles, ironwork, and furniture for several more years.

From left, Malcolm Whitaker, George Pynchon, Alice DeLamar, Lucia Davidova, and George Rand, 1932.

Addison's capacity for work had also been rugged during the years between the Everglades Club and Boca Raton. Yet, after his involvement in the financial disasters that followed, the worry alone must have taken quite a toll. He was broken in spirit as well as literally broke. We may be surprised at all the humor he was able to express in this last manuscript done in those last months of his life. When Harris Drew came to settle his estate, there was very little left to salvage. Actually, it was that very great lady, Edith Oliver Rea, who aided him financially to get through his last year.[16] This is a sad fact.

Alice DeLamar
Palm Beach

Addison Mizner.

Addison Mizner
A Palm Beach Memoir

1

"Never bury an amputated leg laying down. Always bury it standing up, then it will never bother you. If you bury it horizontally then you will never be comfortable. At least that's what my nurse told me when I was a child."

It was Miss Alva talking as she peeked around the corner of my door.[1] She came in hiding behind a huge bunch of yellow chrysanthemums. She was chattering away so fast that I couldn't get in a word edgewise, and she knew that I couldn't reach anything to throw at her.

"If the doctors want your darned old leg, they are going to get it. You know how stubborn they are, so why waste your strength arguing with them?" Miss Alva always took the subjects that no one else dared mention and thrashed them out with you in the most brazen manner.

I had discussed an operation with the surgeon, of course, and only tentatively had he hinted at an amputation. I had flown into a fury, and he dropped the matter.

Miss Alva had made it plain that even if I didn't want to talk about it, my friends had been discussing it freely.

Slowly, I opened my eyes. I was gazing into the face of that nasty, redheaded nurse, the one who had been knitting a sweater using wool rope with flagpoles for needles.

I remember now having asked her if it was for her young man. "Yes," she said. Having asked her what part of the trenches he was in, she had answered, "Oh, he isn't in the trenches; he's stationed in Panama." I don't know why I had ever thought the white lights were the pearly gates. This was Hell, of course.

Heaven has always been so badly advertised. Who wants to sit on a damp cloud, with no Pond's Extract at hand, playing on a harp? I couldn't get a tune out of a Jew's harp.

I felt too sick to care much whether it was Heaven or Hell. At least there would be a lot of people I knew if it were Hell.

Just then, it was a case of "Hasten, hasten, fetch the basin."

I was sick all over with that terrible agony in my left leg that ran clear to the hip.

I must have dozed off for a while, for now my brain was getting clear again. I wasn't dead at all. It was that operation that they had been talking about. I wondered if they had cut off my leg, but I felt too rotten to reach down and find out, or even to ask. Anyway, I hated that nurse and wouldn't ask her anything.

It was all coming back.

Six months ago, in the spring of 1917, I was motoring back from Long Beach late at night. At the drawbridge, as I left the brick-paved street, three young men had asked for a lift. I was driving an open Buick roadster, and they piled in, one sitting on top with his feet hanging down on the seat behind me.

"How far are you fellows going? I turn off at Lynbrook for Garden City. Are any of you going that way?"

"Lynbrook is all right for us," one of them said.

When I got to the place where the road divides, I asked them to tell me where they wanted me to stop.

"Just a block beyond that last light."

In a moment, another one said, "Here."

I slowed down and came to a stop. Just as I did, the fellow behind me grabbed me around the neck, and another one socked me in the eye. My hands were free. I reached for the door latch and with a huge effort wriggled loose and out.

I hadn't had a good look at them before, but as they came in front of the headlights, I saw that they were pretty tough-looking characters. I don't suppose I had a chance from the first, but one fights instinctively. The rotten part was that they had no ethics. One was always behind me, and the long-legged one was trying to kick me where it would most embarrass me. He made two or three near bull's-eyes and then missed entirely, hitting me on my bad ankle.

Twenty-five years before, I had necrosis, or death of the bone, which laid me up in bed and on crutches for five years. For twenty years, I had no trouble with it. But this kick floored me, and I went down like a log. The three of them piled on top of me, and one went through me. A gold cigarette case was the only thing they passed up. They complained bitterly that I only had $29 in cash. A car was coming, and the noble, young fellows jumped the fence and ran into the dark. Instantly, the car picked up and flashed by, showing more sporting bravery.

Finally, on my hands and knees I dragged myself to my runabout and managed to get into the seat. With my right foot I got her started and in agony slowly made the twenty-three miles to Port Washington. At least I could die at home. It was gray in the east. I tooted the horn and then must have fainted. The next I remembered, I was in bed in my own room.

For days, my leg was swollen to the knee. I had been a prisoner in this same room for six months. Yes, it was the same room. There was the huge bunch of chrysanthemums that Miss Alva had brought me only a couple of days ago. How funny she was.

I was drifting back over the past. Only a week before, Wilson, my brother, had arrived with a buck-and-wing dancer who had done his extraordinary dance that shook the floor and jarred my leg to excruciating pain. I couldn't ask him to stop. Wilson had meant it for kindness, and the boy was so earnest about his steps while Wilson beat time on the table.

God, what a relief when they ceased their entertainment and the fellow sat down, all out of breath!

Wilson was my baby brother. We had been more like mother and son all our lives, although there was only a three-year difference in our ages.

"Isn't he great?" he said. "The best in the business. Wait until you see the finale of his act."

I smiled wanly, trying to conceal the fact that one more jounce would kill me.

The lad made some pass just above the knee, unhooked something at the hip, and held up a complicated wooden leg with a shoe and sock on it.

"That's the greatest curtain ever done in vaudeville. Did you ever see anything like it? Only lost his leg three years ago. Would you ever have guessed one of them was phony?"

No one had ever spoken to me about cutting off my leg, except the doctor once, and then I had almost taken his head off. Wilson had been tactful and hadn't mentioned me, but I got what he meant and changed the subject.

It was Miss Alva who had first put it into words.

The room was absolutely silent save for the clicking of those damn knitting needles.

The door opened quietly, and Joseph peered in. He was my butler, and his pretty little wife was the cook. They were both very young, and Germans. I had vouched for them in these war times.

Joseph came over to the bed. He gently took my hand and smiled down at me.

"Did they cut it off, Joseph?"

"No, sir, the doctor said it was going to be all right. This is our lucky day, Mr. Mizner. Hannah just had an eight-pound baby girl, and she's fine, too. We didn't expect it for a couple of weeks, but Hannah got kind of excited about you, and there it was, no trouble at all. I hope you didn't hear it cry."

I hadn't seen Hannah for months and didn't even know she was in a family way. It was all news to me.

In three days, Hannah was back at the stove, and the food was better than ever.

On went the knitting, and I was plotting with Joseph for a gun. I had made up my mind that if the nurse started on mittens and socks for Panama, I was going to kill her.

The house was as silent as a tomb.[2] Mother had died in 1915.[3] One of the boys who made up my household had married, and the other one found it too lonely and moved to New York. I was stark alone and felt it, though my friends were wonderful. They came with books and flowers, and tidbits of gossip.

September and October had dragged by, and now December was battering the windows with cold rains, sleet, and snow.

This was the year of a coal strike, and we were running low. At times, the house was like an icebox, but someway Joseph kept a fire going in my room.

The doctor wouldn't let them talk business to me, and what would be the use—there wasn't any.

Finally, my secretary came out with my lawyer. I saw that they mortgaged the house. Jules Bache and George DeLong had loaned $17,000 on it.

Lady Colebrooke and a young friend of hers named Walter Ogden came out to see me often. Florence Burden drove over almost every afternoon with her Rolls full of firewood, sacks of coal, and all the news of the de Saulles murder trial.[4] She always spent the day at the Mineola courthouse and then came to tea.

December 12th was my forty-fifth birthday. Alex Colebrooke and Walter Ogden came out to have dinner with me and spend the night.[5]

"My dear Addison, you Americans are always spoofing us English about our unheated houses, but this is arctic. Can't they do something about the central heating?"

I rang for Joseph, who I had told Alex was an Alsatian, and asked him to stoke up the furnace.

"There ain't no wood, and there ain't no coal. We cut down the last tree yesterday, but I'm going to pull down the wharf in the morning."

With this embarrassing news he left, returning with an armful of limbs and a small stump.

"You better all stay in here," he said, stirring the coals. He added the evening paper, so it looked warmer anyway.

Alex disappeared for a while and came back blue-nosed.

"I have just had the manager of my apartment house on the line. The little apartment next to mine is vacant, and a car will be here at nine. Ring for your man and let him serve dinner in here. Then, he can get a few things together, and off we go."

We were two hours on the bumpy road in a blizzard before we finally got to Madison and Forty-Eighth Street.

Although I hadn't hobbled further than the bathroom on my crutches, they all somehow managed to get me out of the car and into the apartment. I was exhausted but warm at last.

A Cockney couple ran the place. Syrie Maugham,[6] Alex, and I were all on one floor. I felt as though I had suddenly been transported to Piccadilly.

Walter Ogden had telephoned Wilson to be there to receive me, and he saw how I was suffering. When they got me to bed again, Wilson shooed everyone out.

"God, you look green! Haven't you anything to deaden the pain and make you sleep?"

"No," I said. "They don't believe in it. Aspirin is all they allow me."

"Remember that fellow I got out of jail for smoking opium with the Pearly of Sheepshead Bay? Well, I saw him the other day. He's off the pipe. Said it made too much smell, just like asking the police in. He's taking dope now."

He stepped to the phone and called up a number.

"Hello, that you, Curtis? Say, my brother is in agony. Can you get something for him? All right, come over here. Apartment 3-B. Come right up. Get a hustle on you."

All night long the expert fed me pills. He then gave me stuff to sniff. I got no relief whatsoever, not even a sensation.

"I've been a user for three years, and I don't take as much as that in twenty-four hours," said the hophead. "You must be in agony to stand all that."

I asked Wilson to get me the aspirin and took twenty grains. In ten minutes, I was sound asleep.

I awoke about noon with a pounding headache. Fortunately, I remembered that my expert told me to take plenty of black coffee. This proved an almost instant cure.

Syrie Maugham came in and spent a couple of hours chatting. The room was warm, so I forgot some of my troubles. Alex was in and out.

About four o'clock, Syrie brought in Paris Singer, whom I had met once before.

As he is the cause of my existence for the next ten years, I think I should give you a suggestion of his appearance. He was the finest looking man I ever saw, six feet three or four and straight as a die with a fine figure. At this time, he was fifty and looked forty.

Paris Singer (1867–1932).

He was the twenty-third of twenty-four children and the son of Isaac Merritt Singer, the man who patented the most marketable sewing machine.[7] His father's first wife had two children. Next, he lived with a woman who had ten children, marrying her after his first divorce. He left her for another woman with whom he had five children. Another affair resulted in a daughter before he married Isabella Eugénie Boyer, the mother of Paris. Names had given out, so Papa began naming them after the cities where they were born. In this last litter, the children were: Winnaretta, or Winnie, the Princess Edmond de Polignac; Isabelle, who we called Belle, became the Duchesse Decaze;[8] and then, Washington, Mortimer, Franklin, and Paris.

The old man had patented the most functional sewing machine and had twelve of them ready for sale in 1860. They were big, cumbersome things about the size of a dining room table. He and his partner had about used up their capital and had an awful time selling their output. Finally, by storming the sweatshops of the Lower East Side, they managed to sell the machines. They told each purchaser that as soon as they were in use, and people saw that they could do the work of fifty women, the prices would go up, and they would sell for double the price.

A few months later, the Civil War broke out, and the Singers got a contract for one hundred thousand uniforms. Then, they had to buy back the machines at three and four times the price they had sold them for.

Of course, the fortune was large when the old man's will was settled, and the last batch of children inherited immense legacies. Although he had made sure all his children received a share, the court ruled that his last wife and six children were his legal heirs and entitled to much more than the others.

Most of the last family was born on the other side. When World War I broke out, Paris was virtually "a man without a country." At nineteen, he married a Scotch girl from Australia and had four grown sons and one daughter.[9] Although born in Paris, he lived most of his life in England. His children had been born there and wanted to go into service. So, Paris became a British subject, which automatically made his sons eligible for the army and navy.

Paris had only been to America once before and then only for a couple of months on business. He was about as foreign as could be.[10] Although I had been in England and on the Continent a great deal, I was, after all, just American. Strange to say, we hit it off at once.

Of course, he never understood me, and I doubt if I ever understood him. Paris was a strange, silent man who loved to look on but was hard to talk to unless you got him on his own subjects. At this time, it was hospital work. When the first shot was fired in the world war, he rushed out and bought five hundred beds and everything that went with the most perfectly equipped hospital. Then he telegraphed his doctor to get in touch with a Mrs. Bates. She had taken care of him when he was ill some two years before. He put her in charge of his enormous house in Paignton, located in southwest England.

For several days, the great estate was like a beehive. Within a week, it was readied as the most perfect modern surgical hospital in the world.

Then Paris offered it to the British government, who promptly turned it down, as they had more than enough nursing homes to take care of their possible casualties.

Undisturbed by this rebuff, he went on selecting more equipment.

A few days later, the Battle of the Marne left the world aghast. The government, in a panic, wired him asking if they could change their mind.

On the second day after the battle, ships unloaded twelve hundred wounded at Oldway House in Paignton. Mrs. Bates and Paris were ready.

Joan Bates was the daughter of an English Episcopalian clergyman and an Irish mother. She was born in Shanghai. The "Mrs." title is always bestowed upon the matron of a hospital in England. She inherited the English stolid quality with the Irish humor.

Two years before, a doctor had sent her to Paignton to get things ready for Mr. Singer, who had been taken ill and was to be sent down the next day. She had gone about her work wondering what her patient would be like. In the huge, empty house there was only the caretaker and a cleaning woman. She wondered why the doctor's instructions were that the invalid should be kept quiet. What else could there be but quiet in this great, empty house?

Two motor cars drew up to the door, and Paris got out and handed down Isadora Duncan, a nurse with little Pat,[11] Miss Duncan's brother and his bride of two days,[12] servants, and guests.

Paris was the soul of hospitality and generosity. He had taken the Duncan brother under his wing. He had him appointed to a position in the Singer organization, which would take him to Russia within a few days.

Joan was always businesslike and slapped Paris in bed. She telegraphed the doctor to come and expel the house party.

Three days later, silence reigned again when the caretaker handed Paris a telegram.

"Arrive Paignton four-twenty this afternoon to kill you."

The signature was a single name that he had never heard before. He passed the telegram to Joan.

"Who do you suppose that is, and why does she want to kill me?"

Joan read the message.

"That's the great cinema star—the vamp they call her. I heard Mrs. Duncan say that she would be furious when she heard of the marriage. I really think it would have been courteous of Mr. Duncan if he had broken off his engagement with her before he married Mrs. Duncan."

"Oh, I see. Perhaps, Mrs. Bates, it would be better if you received her and found out just why she is going to kill me. I'm curious, and one can't find out these things after one is killed."

Joan received the great star, whose name was in electric lights over ten thousand movie houses.

The vamp had whipped herself into a frenzy by the time she had arrived. Joan suggested tea while they were waiting for Mr. Singer to come down.

She excused herself to prepare it. In the bottom of the visitor's cup, she poured a few drops of chloral, just to calm the lady's nerves.

The effect was almost instantaneous. The great star got glassy eyed at once. All night long, Joan and the caretaker had to drag her back and forth up and down the passage to keep her from going out entirely.

By morning, the poor woman was so worn out and so mollified that after more black coffee they shipped her back to London without killing Paris, although she was still muttering that she thought it was a dirty trick to help her lover escape to parts unknown in Russia.

Paris recovered rapidly, and Joan went back to London, where two years later she was surprised that Mr. Singer remembered her.

Paris always had the most perfectly pigeonholed mind I have ever known. In an instant, he can tell you the name of the cook who fixes the best spaghetti in Venice or who invented this or that medical instrument.

As soon as the hospital at Paignton was in perfect running order, he went to Paris and established a second hospital at Bellevue and another at St. Cloud.[13] Mrs. Bates got each one into running order with him. He must have spent millions on each.

His present trip to America was twofold. First, he was worn out; second, he was arranging for more finance.

I had only been in my new quarters about a week when Paris came in with a cablegram in his hand.

"Several weeks ago, my solicitor wrote to me that Mrs. Bates was on the verge of a nervous collapse. He could not get her to take a rest, so I let off a wire telling her that I was very ill and asking her if she would come over here and take care of me. I have just got word that she arrives here on Thursday. She has an aunt in New Jersey and one in California, so she can visit them and be quiet. When she arrives, I would like her to have a look at that leg of yours. It shouldn't take such a time to heal. There are so many new things now that she would know. Perhaps, they haven't got here yet. We'll have a try."

There was a great row going on in the hall. There was a knock on the door, and Elsa Maxwell came in with a baby grand piano.[14] For a moment, I couldn't tell which was which.

"I thought some music might cheer you up, so I got these men to move the piano in from Apartment 2-A. The janitor made an awful fuss about letting me do it, but I know the owner won't mind."

"Who does it belong to?" I queried.

"I don't know his name, and he was out, but it's a good piano. I heard him practicing yesterday when I was here," she said in an offhand way. "Got six dollars? I promised these moving men two dollars apiece."

The concert and the piano owner's amazed rage were worth the price.

2

For the next ten days, apartment 3-B was bedlam from noon until midnight. The owner of the piano decided to leave his instrument and joined the crowd. When the door opened, you never knew whether Elsa was bringing in the queen of Romania or an entertainer, and for twelve hours a day, Mayfair, Broadway, and Fifth Avenue were mingled. The bed had been moved into the sitting room, and the nasty nurse slept on a cot in the bedroom.

There was an hour before noon when Paris and I were able to chat. One day I was telling him about Guatemala.

"By Jove, what an extraordinary place. Let's make up a party and go there for a trip. You will all be my guests. I'm tired of war and need a good rest for a few months. What do you say to leaving here about the first of January?"

Anything sounded good to me, and not thinking he was serious, I said yes. Much to my surprise, the next day he bustled in laden down with folders, maps, and tickets.

"Leaving here for New Orleans on January 3rd where we catch the United Fruit boat to Puerta Barrios and then by train to Guatemala City."

He spread open the map and began marking the route and dates.

"By the way, Mrs. Bates arrived yesterday. She seemed a little put out when I met her at the boat, all well and hearty. I told her I wanted her as a consultant for you and that quieted her down a bit. I don't quite like that nurse of yours. Why not let her go, and Mrs. Bates can do the dressing? There are only two of them each day, but that is enough to make her think she is doing something."

I didn't care if Mrs. Bates was a three-toed sloth spitting fire; anything would be better than the nasty nurse, so I said, "Fine."

My leg was healing very slowly. I was as weak as a bridegroom, but I thought a little more practice on my crutches would bring back my old art of getting about with them. But even at that, I wasn't so sure about the trip.

The next morning at eleven, Paris came in with Mrs. Bates and a late paper. Guatemala City had been shaken to the ground by an earthquake, and I sighed with relief.

Mrs. Bates was dressed in a dark, tailor-made suit with a small hat on her auburn head. She was about twenty-eight or thirty and looked very efficient. She took off her gloves and hat. She wanted to see my leg at once. I was sort of embarrassed as she didn't seem like a nurse at all. She was really a great lady. I tried to get off the bandages, but in an instant, she was in full command. She was so gentle and expert that I couldn't help saying, "You're doing it like you were unpacking a rare bit of Greek glass. That stevedore I've had just throws me on the wharf and handles me as though I were a crate of rocks."

She gave me a quick glance of her clear Irish blue eyes. There was a wonderful twinkle in them that literally made us pals for life.

She sterilized and repacked the three slashes before I knew what was happening. I hadn't even looked to see when it was going to hurt. I had been watching her deft hands as they worked with delicacy and decision.

"There now, let me look at you. You are anemic. I'll take a blood test."

In ten minutes, she was putting on her gloves.

"Shall I make a report to you personally, Mr. Singer, or is Mr. Mizner the kind that would like to know things himself?"

I was all for knowing and said so.

"At home one must report to one's doctor, and remember I am not a surgeon. But in my opinion, over there we would build up the patient and expose the wounds to the sun. Is there a solarium that Mr. Mizner could use where they have that new American glass that lets the sun through?"

"You're quite right, Mrs. Bates," said Paris. "When I was here last winter, I slipped down to Palm Beach for a couple of weeks and, as I did not like the hotel, I bought a bit of a villa. It's quite tiny and one of the very few there, but it has four bedrooms and is next to the beach. Now that our Guatemala trip is off, let's go there. Mrs. Bates, would you care to take care of the patient for a month? I think the sunshine would do us all good."

Both Mrs. Bates and I accepted with pleasure. Paris began letting off telegrams to his agent in Palm Beach about electricity, water, and telephones.

On Christmas Day 1917, Lady Colebrook had a tree for Theodore, the head waiter at the Ritz, and his children. I was the only American present.

On January 3, we were all on our way south.

In Paris's cataloged mind, he remembered the Quaco family. Quaco was a butler-valet, and his wife was a cook. Their little girl of four was named Rena.

On the fifth, we arrived at West Palm Beach and found that Paris had bought, by wire, a big Buick touring car, which was waiting. Paris drove, and Joan and I crowded into the backseat with the usual amount of English hand luggage. The Quacos followed in a taxi.

Sunshine never seemed so bright as it glistened on the coconut leaves and sparkled over the lake.

Joan and I thought that little West Palm Beach was Palm Beach. Then, we rattled over a rickety, old, wooden toll bridge into a jungle and onto Peruvian Avenue. There was the great

Atlantic looking like a millpond swish-swashing on miles of perfect beach.

We stopped in front of a little villa, and Paris got out. There were three, lazy-looking women waiting to help open the house. Paris took the keys from the agent and opened the front door.

"Stay where you are, Mizner, until we fix you up."

In a moment, a white iron bed was rolled out on the porch, and they helped me onto it.

Everything was bustle. Paris was in seventh heaven. He was darting out in the car and returning laden with provisions, brooms, and mops, only to give orders and make another sally.

Peruvian Avenue was part of a new development, and like all such things, they had spoiled as much of its natural beauty as possible. Where great jungles had stood, now ragged sand lots stared you in the face. On the next block, on Worth Avenue, was a horrible looking monstrosity called Gus' Bath,[1] and on the front was painted in huge letters, "WELCOME TO OUR OCEAN." Behind this was a cottage with a sign that said Clifton Villa. Next door to our villa were two more atrocities just like the one I was in.

They were development houses. After Paris had an argument with a waiter at lunch at the hotel, he stepped out and bought this one. He dined in his own house and household that night. I was to find that this was typical of him.

I had been alone on the porch for about twenty minutes when there was a shuffling on the boardwalk. Looking up, I discovered the weirdest-looking character I had ever seen. His feet never left the ground. He just shoved along until they had brought him to the foot of the steps.

"Good morning, sir. What butcher are you going to?"

"None, I hope. I've just come from one," I replied, thinking of my operation.

"What grocer are you going to? I'm a professional shopper and can attend to everything for you."

"You'd better go to the kitchen door. I don't know what's going on inside. I'm only a guest."

"Can I do anything for you personally?"

"I'm running low on cigarettes," I said, reaching for my pocketbook. "I'd like a couple of cartons of Moguls."

"You don't need any money. I'll open up an account for you at Speer's Drug Store. What is the name?" said the old man.

I said, "Addison Mizner" and started to spell it out.

"Are you any relation of Mr. Lansing Mizner of San Francisco?"

"Yes, he's a brother."

"The Reverend Henry Mizner of St. Louis?"

"Yes, another brother."

"Then you must be a brother of Mr. Wilson, Mr. Edgar, Mr. William—"

I interrupted him, "How do you happen to know all the family?"

"I was a traveling companion of Mr. Field for over thirty-five years, and he always knew everyone."

I might as well have married the old fellow right then, for he has been with me for the past fifteen years.

"What is your name, sir?" I asked.

"Wendell Wead."

He fascinated me. His stomach ran right to a point, and where a button was missing you could see the deep cavity of his navel. When he chuckled, his stomach would snap rapidly up and down. No belt could hold his trousers up at the right height on that torpedo-pointed front, and pull them up as often as he would, they sagged the minute he let go. Fortunately, his rump was high. The belt disappeared into folds of fat at the back, which securely bolted his pants to him. The festoon effect in front would have otherwise kept you on tenterhooks.

As to age, no one has ever been able to discover. When he first came into my life, I thought he was about seventy, but after fifteen years he now says he is sixty-five. Anyway, he scuffled off to open my first account.

For ten days I lay in the sun, which acted like magic. In three weeks, I was hobbling about quite comfortably on my crutches.

One afternoon I was stretched out on the porch, as usual, when Paris came around the corner of the house.

"What sort of architecture is this?" he asked, as he came up on the porch.

"It must be cotton-back Tibetan," I answered promptly, "for that is the only place in the world I have never been."

"Really," he said, as he disappeared into the house. In a few minutes, he came out with my sketch block, pencils, and watercolors.

"Let's see how it would look silk-back and done correctly."

I looked at him. I have never known to this day when he was spoofing.

Of course, I knew what the house looked like from all angles, for I have a photographic eye. So, I started to work at once. I curled up the corners of the roof and stuck fish on them, in the Chinese manner. I tore off the railing and did something Japanese to it. I was having great fun. With the color box I striped each three rows of shingles a different color, and lacquered posts and panels all over it. No gypsy or Seminole Indian could have got more colors on it, for there were not any more made.

When Paris looked at this sketch, he said, "Quite splendid—I like a bit of color."

I didn't find out for years that he was color-blind and couldn't tell the difference between green and red.

A few minutes later, I heard him start the car and saw him dash out.

It was nearly dinnertime when he returned with the car piled high with ladders, paints, and brushes.

Bright and early the next morning the banging began. A half-dozen carpenters were tearing off the corners of the roof. Paris, himself, was splashing paint on the side of the house, and in his best suit. I was horrified at what I had started. Joan and I went into consultation. She told me he was happiest when he was working, so we decided to say nothing.

The smell of paint and the hammering were awful. So, I took a wheelchair ride.

It was on the North Lake Trail that something happened to my heart. I thought at first that a cannonball had torn through it. The next thing I remember was the wheelchair driver holding me back in the seat.

"You done had a visitation or something," he was saying. "You sure did act up."

There was a bad pain in my heart, but otherwise I seemed all right. I told him to turn around and go home. By the time I got back to the house, I felt all right again and said nothing about my little scare. Joan thought I looked tired, and I turned in early.

The next morning, I had a fearful pain under my left shoulder. When the doctor came, he decided it was pneumonia. I told him about the attack I had. He said it was lucky that the clot of blood had gone through my heart even if it had given me septic pneumonia.

I was pretty sick and wanted to doze all the time. About the third day, I think it was, I heard a low buzz of conversation.

"I wired Walter Ogden yesterday to come down. He may know whether Addison has any family to notify. Ferguson's Funeral Home say they haven't a casket big enough. Do you think I should tell them to order one out of Atlanta?" This was all in Paris's voice.

Joan said, "Doctor Downs[2] says there is one chance in a hundred, so we had better wait. The crisis will probably be tonight."

I rang the bell. Paris and Joan came in. I said in a rather gasping voice, "Don't you think the Mizners are well enough brought up to know it's rude to die in somebody else's house? I'll be all right in a day or so."

And I was. I didn't need the oversized casket. In fact, I haven't had to wear one yet.

3

Convalescence was rapid. Within ten days I was taking short motor rides. On my second outing, Paris stopped the car to watch the surf advance and retreat on a stretch of beach where the Kingsley house[1] now stands.

"This would be a lovely place for a villa right on the sands. What do you see here?" he said.

I closed my eyes and answered, "A Moorish tower, like on the south coast of Spain with an open loggia at one side facing the sea. And on this side, a cool court with a dripping fountain in the shade of these beautiful palms."

We drove on in silence, returning to the Tibetan atrocity. The fish I had drawn for the roof hadn't turned out to Paris's liking, so he purchased five-foot stuffed alligators in their stead. There they pranced on the roof in their shiny spar varnish to defy good taste. The whole thing was so funny that I had to laugh and quickly think of something to tell Paris so he wouldn't know I was laughing at the house.

A couple of young aviators from the Miami Flying School were waiting for me on the porch. Joan was entertaining them, and they were all laughing as we drove up.

Paris drove into the garage and did not join us, which I thought odd. Dinner was announced, and Joan asked the boys to stay, which they had intended to do anyway.

Paris stamped in and was introduced. His manner was very stiff, almost rigid. "I'm dining out," he said. He gave Joan a dirty, dignified look and was gone.

We dined merrily, although it was like Hamlet without little Eva. Once or twice, I caught a puzzled look in Joan's eyes.

La Billucia, 1200 South Ocean Boulevard. North elevation with elaborate entrance.

Paris returned, went upstairs, and then out again. He did this three or four times before the boys left, and I wondered what they thought. When the boys left, Joan asked, "Whatever do you suppose is the matter with Mr. Singer? He seemed very angry, and it wasn't because I asked those boys to dinner. In all the hospitals he has established, one of the first rules he made was that any visiting soldier must be asked to stay for lunch or dinner. It couldn't have been that. What do you suppose it is?"

"Jealousy," I answered.

"Over what, and likewise whom?" Joan queried with eyes wide open.

"You, poor dub! Haven't you seen the signs growing in the last couple of weeks? I've been a love expert for others for years. Although I haven't made a success of it myself, I know the symptoms in others."

Joan scoffed at the idea.

"Don't be silly. Mr. Singer and I have worked together since the beginning of the war, and he has never known I was anything but part of a machine. We've both been too busy for that."[2]

"That's just it. He hasn't been so busy in the past few months."

"Absurd! And besides he's in love with someone else."

"He was, you mean."

I knew she meant Isadora Duncan. I thought of Bernard Shaw's reply to her when she asked to have a child by him:

"Just think of an offspring with your mind and my body," she had pleaded. He is supposed to have replied, "Just think of an offspring with your mind and my body."

The next morning, I said, "I hope you didn't mind my asking the boys to dinner last night, Paris. I have known them since they were babies. I'm sorry."

"Quite all right, quite all right."

By noon, everything was all hunky-dory again. At teatime, he announced that he had bought the site for the Moorish tower, and I had to make sketches.

The next day we drove down by the lake, where Worth Avenue begins to turn into Lake Drive. The mullet were jumping in the sunset, and hundreds of egrets were making their way home to their rookery on Lone Cabbage Island.

"What do you see on this site?" Paris asked.

"It's so beautiful that it ought to be something religious—a nunnery with a chapel built into the lake with great cool cloisters and a court of oranges. A landing stage, where the stern old abbess could barter with boatmen bringing their fruit and vegetables for sale. And a great gate over there on the roof, where the faithful could leave their offerings and receive largess."

"It could be a mixture, built by a nun from Venice, added onto by one from Gerona, with a bit of New Spain of the tropics. What a spot!"

We watched the day die in its tropical glory and went home in silence, each dreaming his own dream.

Two days later, Paris had bought the property, nearly a half mile wide and running through from the ocean to the lake. He started the Ocean and Lake Realty Company, and I was made president.

It was spring here, and hundreds of mockingbirds and cardinals were bursting with song. I had thrown away my crutches and was feeling fine. I felt I should make some pretense of going home, as it was the end of March.[3] Guests at the hotels were thinning out, and the season was over on Washington's Birthday. I thanked Paris for his extraordinary hospitality and apologized for my pneumonia.

"I say, old man, you can't leave me here to manage this realty company. You're the president and drawing a salary." He mentioned a sum that, although not big, was better than going back to New York and uncertainty.

"As you know, I have several hospitals on the other side and none here. Father made his start in America, and I have been

Everglades Club and Villa, 1918. Original clubhouse west elevation with Venetian Terrace overlooking Singer Basin.

thinking that I should do something here for your soldiers as well. How about building a hospital for shell-shocked soldiers down on the lake? It's so peaceful and quiet there that the boys couldn't help getting well in a jiffy."

We talked for hours about the possibilities. I was all enthusiasm, but even then, I didn't think of it having a possibility. Although the gardener always referred to the company as the Ocean and Lake Realty Company, it was not until Singer bought a house over on the railroad tracks in West Palm Beach and opened an office that I began to think of it seriously.

Joan had been doing the housekeeping and complained that you couldn't get a fresh vegetable in the state; even the milk was condensed in a can. She put this up as a drawback for a hospital. The next day after this argument, Paris bought several hundred acres located two miles in the Everglades[4] and said he was going to start a truck garden and dairy there.

April came, with its great flights of millions of dragonflies, and then the mosquitoes.

One day at lunch I happened to say, "This would have been a good warm day for ice cream. I meant to have stopped at Speer's and bought some on my way home."

Joan said, "We ought to have a freezer."

Paris interrupted her with, "The Quacos have got enough to do without that," and then the conversation flopped.

Several days later, we had ice cream.

"Where did this come from?" Paris asked.

Joan promptly lied, "Mrs. Clifton sent it over," so nothing further was said. Directly after lunch, he went into the kitchen and found a shiny, new freezer that had been sent over from Guild's Furniture Store and had cost $2.35. Then the battle of the ice-cream freezer broke out. He came storming back and insulted Joan until she fled to her room and locked herself in. She didn't come out for three days. And then, only when railroad tickets were slipped under her door, and she was told she could go home.

It had been dreadful, and my love theory began to weaken.

We three dined alone. I was used as a telephone through which each could insult the other by making remarks to me. Dinner was over early. The servants had piled the back of the car with Joan's parcels and other luggage.

"It's an hour before train time. We shall drive the ocean road before we go to the station."

It was an order, not a request, from Paris. It was dark by now, and we sped along. At the turn of the road, where Harold Vanderbilt's house now stands,[5] there was a crash.

"What's that?" I asked and turned to Joan, seated among her boxes on the backseat.

"Did you hear something?" she asked.

"Probably, we ran over a palm leaf, that's all," I answered.

We finally turned around and made for the station. I handed Joan out, and a porter took her traps.

"Good-bye, Mr. Singer. I'm sorry."

She held out her hand, which he overlooked. He said a curt good-bye, driving off at breakneck speed.

Joan turned to me. "Of course, you know what that crash was, don't you?"

"No, what was it?"

"The ice-cream freezer. I just dropped it out. He had it all nicely wrapped up for me to take with me."

"Well, I give up. As a love expert. I'm a bust."

"Not altogether. He's been making love to me for weeks, and I pretended I didn't understand. The morning we had ice cream he told me he loved me. I told him that was an insult as he hadn't gotten a divorce. You know for the past twelve years it has only been a separation. Well, he's just a big, spoiled boy, and he hates to be put in the wrong."

The train came in, and I helped her into her compartment. The train was starting as I got off. Paris dashed up in his car yelling to stop the train. He was waving the freezer.

"Put this in Mrs. Bates's room," he called.

The train was well under way by the time Paris had stopped the motor and I had reached the car.

"Let's go home. I'm tired and I have to be at the farm at seven to see about the clearing."

We went back in silence.

Next morning, when I came home for lunch, I found Paris packing the freezer ready to send it to Joan in care of her New Jersey aunt.

"She'll just send it back. Between the two of you, you'll wear the damned thing out," I kidded him into putting it back into the kitchen.

The rest of the day we didn't mention Joan. The following day, Paris said, "Isn't it great, not having a woman around? Now we can get something done."

About six that afternoon he came into my room. "Can you get ready to catch the seven-twenty train? I've got to go to New York on business, and I want you along to look at dairy equipment, plumbing, and a lot of other things."

I was always ready to go anywhere and said so.

He spent most of the trip letting off telegrams. When we arrived at Penn Station the next evening, there were twenty or thirty people to meet him. His secretary was a charming woman, who I knew to be very fond of Joan.

"What's all the excitement?" I asked her.

"He's been telegraphing apologies to Joan. She wouldn't answer them, so he came up to try and smooth things over. Joan took a noon train to California when she heard he was coming."

They were just two kids. I was disgusted. I had left my work just at the start, and I was mad.

A machine-gun fire of telegrams was let off as a barrage of telephoning began. Joan was stopping over in Chicago, and Paris left me flat to retrieve his beloved, with the aid of the entire staff of the sewing machine world.

I went to Port Washington and packed up my furniture, sold the house, paid the mortgage, and waited.

Under the chaperonage of the secretary, Joan came back to stay with her aunt in New Jersey. Evidently, some understanding had been reached because Paris and I went back to Palm Beach. We had lost a month, and it would be no joke to get through by the season, for it was now the middle of June. I picked up two men as draftsmen. One was fair, and the other was very medium.

It took me some time to convince Paris that it would be better to build something well. That is, out of fireproof construction instead of a makeshift material. It was the first of July before we had decided to do something that could be used as a club when the war was over.

Finally, he OK'd a very rough sketch of the Everglades Club and left for New York on business, which I knew was light courting. The afternoon of his departure, we roughly staked out the main building. It was the 10th or 12th of July 1918.

Two days later, I started foundations. I had roughed it in Alaska and built the first business buildings in Dawson with unskilled labor. I plunged in, thinking it couldn't be worse than that. The difference was apparent at once. No one wanted to work. All the able-bodied men had gone to war, and those who were left had hookworm. To illustrate the energy of the native, the following experience is necessary.

I had bought a sawmill about fifteen miles north of town and had to superintend it. I drove up after lunch, along the narrow Dixie Highway, and met a man in a big wagon with two horses, herding a lot of pigs before him. Of course, I had to stop

Chateau Myscene, Port Washington, New York. First known as the Baxter Homestead, Mizner rechristened his Long Island residence after making additions and alterations.
Mizner Library Foundation

the car, and we both got out to shoo the grunters by. Four hours later, when I was returning, I overtook the same party, who had not covered much more than a mile. And again, I had to go through the same tactics. As the man climbed back into his seat, I asked him, "Why don't you put the pigs in the wagon? You'd make much better time."

"What the hell is time to a hog?" came back from the dreary philosopher.

From that moment, I realized what I had to deal with.

In Palm Beach, there were fewer than thirty little, shingled houses. As they cooked on kerosene stoves, there was no need for a chimney. Therefore, no one had ever met a brick in their lives and didn't know how to act with one. First of all, I was running a trades' school, for I had to teach them how to lay brick. When the first car of hollow building tile was delivered to the job, I found my entire crew chasing a skunk back and forth through the holes. My mason looked up and said, "What the hell are them things for?"

"Not to catch skunks in, anyway. Get to work. I'll show you."

The living room was to be where the old alligator farm was; it had been sold with the property.[6] So I became the president of a sea cow and twelve hundred alligators, several rattlesnakes, and other pets for which I had to build new quarters.

At first, Paris took over The Novelty Works at the lumber company for construction materials to build the club before we set up our own workshops on South Dixie Highway. Nowhere could I get tile for my roofs, so I built kilns and imported clay from Georgia. I took over a blacksmith shop and made light fixtures, andirons, and ornamental gates and grilles. I made furniture in one of the workshops.[7]

I built a barn for 120 cows and had to act as envoy in negotiating for their husbands. I established a chicken farm and went into raising pigeons.

Running an architect's office was no fun because no one could read plans and thought blueprints were some sort of game.

The business office was also hard, as Mr. Singer bought new property on each visit, and titles had to be searched and accounts kept.

Then there were fresh vegetables to be thought of and gardens to supply cut flowers. Also, I had to go into the nursery business and build a tree-moving machine, or a derrick on wheels. In fact, that summer I was kept more or less busy with strikes and politics.

A man named Joe Earman ran the *Palm Beach Post*. At first, I was on friendly terms with him. He sat in his office behind a golden oak desk with a huge, cheap safe at his elbow, which was labeled in huge letters, "Hell Box." It supposedly held

Mizner Industries, Bunker Road, West Palm Beach. The pottery and roof tile kilns and production facilities were located at the center of Mizner Industries that extended from Bunker Road north to Putnam Road and from Webster Avenue west to Norton Avenue.

something detrimental about everybody in the state. He was, at that time, the head of politics and gave himself great airs. In reality, he was the slimiest old joke I have ever seen.

Things had begun to run more smoothly at the buildings when a strike was declared. I consulted Earman and found that he was on the side of the voters, regardless of principle or progress. I got Paris on the wire, and we decided to meet the demands.

One night, when I was returning from the movies in old "Beulah Buick" during the strike, I was stopped by a man on Royal Palm Way. Beulah was in a pretty bad way. One door was gone, and my batteries had run so low that half the time I had to crank her. As I stopped to see what the man wanted, four others came out of the jungle and began the battle. It was so sudden and unexpected that they crowded me back into Beulah.

My hand, going back to keep me from falling, struck the crank. I began doing a Spanish dance with it, cracking the one and swinging on that, until I had three strikes and the other two fled.

Next day, I sent an emissary to the hospital, who identified three of the men as strike leaders. I was never quite sure who the other two were.

What fun it all was, showing men how to stucco, teaching others how to cure pip in chickens, clearing jungles, killing land crabs with gas, catching new alligators in the Everglades, and planning ahead for every little detail to be ready to slip into place. It was all like a game.

Paris was coming down for a few weeks at a time, working like a dog, improving this, and suggesting that, seeing every day, story after story piled up higher and higher, while gardens were growing, cows were breeding, and tiles burning.

In New York, Paris was as busy as I was down here. He sent out fifty thousand invitations to wounded men to come and recuperate at the Everglades Rod & Gun Club. He formed committees and a board of governors. Things were bowling along.

One November morning, at about three, the Quacos came bursting into my room. "The Bosh are bombing West Palm Beach," they shrieked.

I rushed out in my pajamas, started old Beulah, and scooted over the bridge.

It was the armistice.[8]

4

Of course, no one came to work that day, and it gave me time to worry as to whether the armistice would end my Florida career.

That night I got Mr. Singer on the phone. He seemed surprised and indignant that I would even think such a thing.

"If we start things off right, it will make Palm Beach the winter capital of the world. There is no place in Europe to compare with the climate. All that is needed is to make it gay and attractive. It's up to you and me. There are hundreds of thousands of wounded who will need us besides. Do not forget that," he said over the phone.

Things were beginning to fit together now. The club itself had a huge living room, a dining room that would seat four hundred, and twelve bedrooms. There was a big tower with a suite that I had arranged for myself, where Mr. Singer also had an apartment. There were also seven other buildings, each with eight rooms, and the medical building, which had the most perfect equipment ready to be installed.

Just before Christmas, a few people began to arrive. For months, the locals had stopped to criticize, saying, "Oh, my God, it ain't anything like the Poinciana or The Breakers. Ain't it awful?" It was the snowbird or winter visitor whose criticism I feared.

I had one admirer who was faithful. Every day at eleven thirty a big limousine arrived with an old man and a very handsome woman one-half his age, with a beautiful expression. They would get out and pass the sign, Positively No Admittance, like a dirty deuce in a new pack.

The first time I noticed them, I asked the man who should have stopped them who they were. Above the hammering and other din, I only heard the words, "great politician." So, I went over, more or less with the idea of throwing them out. The old man bowed, and before I could be rude, said, "The most magnificent proportions I ever saw. Who is the architect?"

It was the first criticism that was not adverse. I fell on his neck and asked him to have lunch with me at the Tibetan villa. He then introduced his young wife. The couple fascinated me, so I drew the clerk of the works aside, who said, "Why, that's Boss Croker and his Indian wife."[1]

I was horrified, as for years I had seen Nast's bitter cartoons and heard of Richard Croker. As a child hears of the boogie man, I had asked this dragon to lunch.

There was always a great deal of ceremony about Daddy, as his wife called him. With the greatest dignity, he arrived.

It couldn't be, for this was the sweetest old fellow I had ever met, simply radiating charm. Bula, or Mrs. Croker, was charming, too. The old man had twinkling blue eyes, so witty and amusing. I was fascinated.

They were the first people I had entertained for months, and I flopped completely. For three solid months they lunched with me, or I with them. I grew to admire them both more and more as time went on.

It was weeks before I discovered the reason that they were staying down all summer. It was a continuous lawsuit brought by his greedy children, who were trying to put their father in an asylum and grab his money.

The case came up, and every second that I could get off was spent at their counsel's table with them. The publicity had been bad, for the papers made it appear that Daddy had married Bula only a few days after the death of his wife. This was true, but they carefully neglected to say that he had been separated from his first wife for nearly twenty years and that the old man had settled two-thirds of his estate on his wife and children and gone to live in Ireland.

One morning, they had a doctor on the stand who qualified as an insanity expert. He sat there slowly revolving a stiff straw hat and trying to look erudite.

"Why do you think, doctor, that Mr. Croker is insane?" the defense asked.

"Any old man who marries a young wife is insane."

"Have you examined Mr. Croker? How well do you know him?"

"I've seen him twice. Yesterday afternoon, I said, 'Good day' to him, and he answered me. This morning, I did the same."

"Is that the only conversation you have had with him?"

"Well, yes. He doesn't seem to care to talk to me."

The testimony had gone on in this manner for an hour when Daddy tiptoed up to his counsel and whispered something.

"Mr. Croker wants to know what size hat you wear?"

"Why, six and a half!"

"You're excused," said the defense. The room echoed with laughter.

Of course, you know that you couldn't get a six-and-a-half hat on a dodo bird's head.

One evening, I was on the balcony of my new apartment in the tower when I saw a white figure far below.

"Hello! Is that you, Mizner?"

"Yes, who's that?"

"John King,"[2] came back the answer. "Can I come up?"

"Certainly! The elevator isn't running, but come in the door just under me and hit the stairs."

Blowing and puffing, John arrived.

"My heavens, man, this is the most beautiful thing I ever saw. I don't feel as though I was in America; might be in Italy or Spain. It's wonderful."

I began to feel like I was looking like a pouter pigeon, I was getting so swelled up.

"Are you under contract to Singer? Can you do any outside work at all?"

I thought I smelled a job coming, although I knew he had a little colonial house under some coconut trees that looked as much at home as a cow in a hummingbird's nest. Perhaps he now sensed it and was going to build a palace.

"No, I'm not exactly under contract," I said cautiously. "I can do other work."

"That's great! Can you come up about teatime tomorrow? I want you to design me a bicycle rack."

I was sure somebody had stuck me with a hat pin, and I could hear the wind just hissing out of me.

But I went for tea and designed the bicycle rack.

The Everglades Club was to open February 4, and it was early in January that my dredge broke down. There was to be a large terrace in the angle between the living room and the dining room with steps down into the lake. It was still only a sump hole with walls and steps at the far corner, but no fill, only two huge concrete septic tanks floating about in the enclosure. I finally had to give a party for the local fire engine company and get them to fill my tanks until they sank. Then I anchored them, and my guests pumped them out again. But the terrace was not so easy.

Paris had arrived with a staff for the club. Everyone drove me crazy with, "Oh, we'd better put off the opening for a year" and the like.

Luck was with me. A dredge was going through to work on the canal, and I bribed the tug man to break down in front of the club. Before they could get it fixed, they had poured my terrace.[3]

My huge royal palms were all root pruned, as were the orange trees, and we moved them in one night. I had been soaking my grass seed in warm water for two days, and they started to sprout as I raked it in.

The night before the opening, I bought a dozen crates of oranges and as many boxes of hairpins. By morning, the trees were hanging heavy with fruit.

I was dead on my feet. As the first guests arrived, I sank down behind some palms to try to hear some unbiased criticism.

Craig Biddle and Birdie Vanderbilt were within three feet of me.[4] They couldn't have been more complimentary had they known I was listening in. My heart went out to them. In fact, there were few knockers. I sneaked up to my rooms in a trance of pleasure.

People had said, "No one will go way down there in the jungle. Singer and Mizner are crazy."

But it became the very right place to go and was crowded.

One day I caught Mrs. Edward T. Stotesbury stepping off the width of terraces. I went over and offered to help her.

"Oh, Mr. Mizner, you have made me so discontented with the plans I have had done for El Mirasol,[5] I don't think I will ever be content with them after seeing this."

I had seen the plans a year before and knew she wouldn't if I could help it.

"I must talk to Mr. Stotesbury about you, and perhaps we will ask you about a few changes."

I saw I had her hooked and gave the line a few deft jerks.

Gurnee and Charles Munn both decided to build and came to me for plans, as did E. Clarence Jones.[6]

I had not thought of staying on at Palm Beach, but why not? I was in love with the place, and Mr. Singer had fired me with a dream, so I took the jobs.

I saw at once that I was dealing with the rich and would have to invent something big for as little money as possible. The argument always was, "You know we will only use a house here three or four weeks a year, so we don't want a big investment."

The Munn houses were easy. We rapidly came to an agreement as to price and plan, and they were let out to contract.[7]

Mrs. Stotesbury was a little harder. She was accustomed to great wealth and thought nothing of a few little changes. I soon got to calling her Mrs. Simon Legree, as we bantered along good-naturedly.

Most people think that if they criticize the work of an artist—I use the word as a generality—they will get something better next time, where, as a matter of fact, nine times out of ten, you kill any inspiration an artist might have. So, I got Mrs. Legree's mind concentrated on the front elevation and used more spit changing the watercolor sketch of the east front than I had ever done before.

A doctor has such an advantage over an architect. He can chloroform his patient and do as he likes. I determined to use my own anesthetic, for when I bade my patients adieu at the end of the season, I didn't expect to see them again until the operation was over. Early in life, I found a formula: never disagree with a client, but if you don't like their suggestion, pretend you think they are great, then look thoughtful, and say, "Yes, I like your idea very much." Then pause, and say, "But you know, I think I like your first idea best." Of course, they have never had a first idea in their lives. But one can rapidly sketch their own ideas out as well as possible, and then do an awful thing of the patient's new idea and lay them side by side.

Make them think it is their thought and it generally goes, for most of them will not try to remember thinking anything, forget what they have been talking about, and drop the subject. Most people know that they can't paint a portrait, cut off a leg, or build up a law case, but everyone thinks they are a better architect than you are.

If I have had any success at all, it is because my clients took their ether by going away for eight months and coming back when the operation was over.

"I think your ideas have worked out wonderfully," was always my greeting, and this sort of stops them.

All this is not directed at Mrs. Stotesbury but is just in the way of giving a helping hand to poor architects, and I don't care how you take poor. As a matter of fact, Mrs. Legree and I got on beautifully, and I enjoyed working with her immensely. Of course, she moved a partition or two, but she knew what she wanted.

One incident concerned her bathroom. There are only three pieces of furniture that must go in, and we made seven different arrangements of these before things looked right. Then, she decided to move her sitting room over to where her bathroom was and make the sitting room the bathroom.

Out of forty years of practice, I have only had one real row with a client, and I think this is a record.

This was with E. Clarence Jones, who had been a gentleman friend of my twice-removed sister-in-law of a few minutes, Mrs. Yerkes.[8]

Jones had come from a rather obscure beginning and made a wad, and the old sow's ear fitted him perfectly. He gave me a job to do a house, with furniture, gardens, and all complete for $10,000. Owing to strikes and a heavy rise in material costs, it couldn't be done, so I put in $3,000 of my own to make good. There were no specifications as to furniture, and I must say the house was not a museum, but it was comfortable and rather attractive for the price.

He seemed pleased with it all and asked me to add to the furnishings. Together we made out a list of what he wanted added, which came to $2,400 at Guild's Furniture Company in West Palm Beach. The new things were delivered on the 14th of January. On the first of February, I was going into the Stotesbury's and passed a deputy sheriff. I stopped to have a few polite words with him. I had no sooner gotten down to working on a few changes with Mrs. Stotesbury before the sheriff came in and presented me with a service.

It was a subpoena. Guild's was suing me for $2,400 for the Jones's furniture, which I had bought in my own name to save a discount for Jones. I left Mrs. Legree and caught up with the deputy. "Why didn't you hand me this at the gate?" I asked.

"Mr. Jones said he would give me twenty-five dollars if I would serve you before the Missus Stotesbury."

I was furious. I felt I couldn't have people suing me in my first real year of practice. I went back to Madame and soon finished my work with her. Then, I went on to my office.

I was building a house for myself, and my checkbook was pretty flat. But, by stopping the work on my house I was able to make out a check in full payment. I went over to Guild's still in a rage and slapped down the check on Mr. Frederick Guild's desk.

"Give me a receipt," I demanded.

When he made it out, I opened up with my tirade, calling him out of his name and winding up with, "I hope you drop dead right where you stand."

I was having tea with Marie Louise Munn and a dozen others. I was so full of the rottenness of the whole situation that I told the whole thing in detail.

Several days later, Marie Louise rang me up.

"Have you seen the papers?" she asked. "Guild dropped dead at his desk yesterday afternoon, just where you told him to."

I was shocked. Having no superstitions, I soon got over it and forgot it entirely—that is, until a year later when one of the women who had been at the tea the day I talked about it asked if I would pray her stepmother to death.

Murder was one commandment I didn't even want to scratch. But I saw a way out. One always hears the gossip. Mrs. Grundy had it that the stepmother had fallen in love with a much younger Englishman and that the father was going to get the slide anyway.

Evidently, my client had not heard the rumor. I pretended to go into a trance and promised her that her stepmother would go out of her life within six months, and she did.

So, I had several clients the next year.

Barnum was right, and building houses wasn't their only foolishness.

5

I had put in a lot of time and thought into my tower apartment at the club. But father was right: "If you are so stupid you have to stop to think, it's better not to think at all."

The apartment was a bust. For it was in the club, and one of the board of governors was E. Clarence "Swillcan" Jones. At their very first meeting, my two chow dogs were ruled out. This was divorcing me from my dear ones. At the next meeting, they ruled, "Ladies are not admitted above the first floor." I was five flights up.

E. Clarence had won the first round. The club had snapped its door on my behind. I took a house on the oceanfront. Then, I bought a slice of property a mile south of Gus' Bath and started a tiny house of my own.[1]

People said I had lost my reason entirely to go way off in the jungle, but I felt sure that things would spread out and catch up with me in time. Besides, I rather liked the idea of privacy. Anyway, they thought me mad when I had built the club, and now it was the center of things.

Charlie Christmas was a delightful old man who worked for me at the club. The club had used him as furnace man, but, of course, let him go when it closed for the season.

One morning I heard a row near the club kitchen and went to see what the trouble was. The swill man had not come.

"Charlie, why in hell don't you use that incinerator I built?"

"Why Mr. Mizner, these incinerators stir up such a stink."

Knowing that he was a philosopher, I dropped the subject.

"Where is Mr. Singer?" I asked him one morning.

"Oh, Mr. Singer is out in the percolator."

As Paris was often steaming hot about trivialities, I didn't look for him.

Charlie always, winter or summer, inside or out, wore an old brown derby jammed down to his ears, which seemed so dressy when he was pushing a wheelbarrow. He liked to rest. He would always set down his barrow when he saw me and start gabbing.

"Why, Mr. Mizner, this house of yours is getting more palacy every day."

Charlie's eyes rolled about in their sockets.

"I'd like to get tomorrow off, sir. You know my divorce is coming up."

"Your divorce? You have had two already this year. What's the matter, don't you think matrimony is a good thing?"

"No," he said, hesitatingly, as though in great thought. "Marriage ain't good 'cept for one thing, and I guess it cheaper at that to get your washing done outside."

So, I have remained a bachelor because Charlie was nearly always right. I finished my house guest-proof and wife-proof. I hired Mrs. Anna Mae Srumeger to do the honors and sent my washing to the Chinese laundry.

Mae was under five feet, with masses of red hair and freckles. She had come from the mountains of Tennessee with an old mother. She worked herself into a wire spring trying to take care of her and was delighted to have a job for the summer.

By the middle of July, we moved into El Solano.[2]

When my mother died in 1915, all communication with the rest of the family ceased. My five brothers and one sister wrote only to their mother. Although I had only seen one or two of them in nearly twenty years, I was mildly interested to hear of their doings. Even if we had been more intimate, it would have been impossible to correspond with six people. To write snappy letters to people one hardly knew was out of the question, so we let the matter drop.

Late in the winter of 1919, I got a letter from my sister Min saying that little Horace had just returned from abroad, where he had been with the Canadian Flying Service.[3] She asked me if I would step across the street into New York from Palm Beach and look him up.

It seemed impossible. For only yesterday, when I had last seen him in Rome, he was scarcely out of diapers. And now, he was returning from the war. Was it possible?

I took the train north the next night. Horace had moved, and I spent two days trying to find him. Finally, I located him as a mechanic in a garage. Tall, blond, and slender, he was a fine-looking lad of twenty. But, oh so sloppy! I fed him for an hour and a half, took him to a tailor and haberdasher, and then, sat down to hear his story.

The family had lost their magnificent country place, which was one of the biggest vineyards in California, when Prohibition came in.[4] The rest of the fortune had been in Mexican mines, which went to pot when President Diaz blew up and revolution again took the country. We talked things over for a couple of days, waited for new clothes, and started south.

It was the first time I had heard of the family reverses. I was worried about what to do with the kid and began trying to dope out a job for him.

When I had been president of the Ocean and Lake Realty Company, I had run ten or more distinct companies. These took in real estate, architecture, contracting, sawmills, furniture shop, and even spent time milking a sea cow at the alligator farm. When the Everglades Club was finished, Mr. Singer ordered me to dispose of most of them, which I did at a profit, after getting everything at cost and much below market prices.

But there was one left. This was the pottery. There was no way of figuring out whether it was a winner or a loser, as we were making something that could not be bought in the USA, to wit: handmade roof tiles. All the commercial ones were stamped out and looked like painted tin when they were laid. They were a horrible lurid color that made a roof look like the floor of a slaughterhouse. I took over this property in the following way.

Paris was just a big, spoiled youngster. When I had gone to him saying that the Stotesburys wanted me to build for them, he was delighted. But, as he thought things over, he began to think I was stepping away from him and was going to have all the fun without letting him play with the blocks, too. He got jealous and told me he was going to shut down the pottery. This was a staggerer, for what's a Spanish house with a tin roof? But I said nothing, got up the statement, and turned it in. It came to a little over $14,000, and that was that. I floundered around to see what I could do in getting tiles from Cuba.

It always annoyed poor Paris that I wouldn't argue with him. By the end of a couple of weeks, having stood my acquiescence as long as he could, he said, "What are you going to do about tiles?"

"I have made arrangements with the lumber yard and Mr. Kelsey at Kelsey City, and we are going to put up kilns there."

Of course, this was a lie, but I had to say something.

"Why don't you buy my plant?"

As the first payment was only the price of the stamps on the deed, I said, "Fine. What's the price?"

"Cost of land, machinery, et cetera."

It was at this time I found out for the first time you could borrow from a bank on a note. I thought they were like pawnshops, and as I had nothing to hock, I was surprised.

So, Mizner Industries, Incorporated, began under the name of Las Manos Potteries. We started clapping the tiles on roofs so hot the men could hardly handle them and were paid cost plus 20 percent on delivery. That was that.

Now Horace was to run that end while I went on with architecture and contracting.

I added an extra room to the house, and the most untidy war hero in the world moved in with me. Having been a tidy old bachelor for so long, it nearly drove me crazy opening Horace's door and finding his shoes on the bureau and his shirt on the floor. But he was the best-natured slob I ever saw, and we soon came to an agreement that restricted his messiness to his own room.

By now, I was building many houses, and one of my clients asked me to store several thousand dollars' worth of liquor in his unfinished basement. The goods were delivered one night and sealed up.[5] Several days later, I drove up to the job, to be stopped by Charlie Christmas, just before I got into the gate.

"My gawd, Mr. Mizner, that place is just swarming with them government lice. You better act like a groundhog and burrow in somewhere!"

Someone had tipped off the federal Prohibition agent, and they were after me. I took it on the run for my own cellar, but Anna Mae had beat me to it. She had been shoveling coal for an hour or so.

Ten days before this happened, Horace had gone swimming in front of the house. It was mid-September, and the equinox storm was at its height. Above the crash of the waves, I heard a call for help, as did Anna Mae and a young friend of Horace's.[6] We all started running for the beach and dragged Horace out on the sand. His leg was hanging only by the bone, as the flesh from knee to ankle was flapping on tiny hinges. A shark had grabbed him and only by a miracle had he beat it off. It's funny how things strike one. Horace had gone down to the beach in only a dressing gown, and as we dragged him along, I was thinking about Anna Mae's attitude toward nakedness.

While I got on a tunic, Mae telephoned for doctors. Bob hopped in my car and went for a nurse. In half an hour, the house was full, and everyone was praying. Having put up a battle to save my own leg, I gave my ultimatum. One of the doctors had just returned from the war and knew something of Dakin's solution. He gave the prescription over the phone, and another dash was made to West Palm Beach.

For two hours they knitted, herringboned, crocheted, and embroidered until they had used up all the catgut for a radius of ten miles. The poor kid was a Spartan. He must have suffered the tortures of the hereafter but tried to joke from first to last. God, he had grit!

Of course, there was no sleep for me. I spent the night prowling about the house with a bundle of cotton and a bucket of peroxide cleaning blood off my new stone steps and heretofore spotless walls. He was out of danger of blood poisoning but still very white and weak when the police broke in.

Before I drew the bolts, I sneaked up and told him to look sicker. As I opened the door a Roman mob tried to jam in. I forced them back and invited the chief and his first assistant to enter, inquiring about what was the matter and what I could do for them. I was standing in the hall next to the dining room door when I felt something rapping me on the hip. It was Mae whispering, "Shoot the dirty rats in the belly" as she tried to slip an old six-shooter into my hand.

I was so polite and forlorn about my dying nephew that after a tiptoed search of only half an hour, I kissed them out, as I was presented with a warrant to appear in Miami.

My feelings were divided between pride of being the first man in America to be arrested on a liquor charge or being terrified of the man they left at the door with a rifle.

I soon arranged over the telephone $3,500 bail. Several weeks later, I appeared before the judge, who let me off with a $250 fine and a reprimand.

By the way, my client in whose basement the booze had been found only had $50 million. He let me pay the fine and my lawyer's fee.

6

One of the greatest sights of Palm Beach was the Jungle Trail, a place where the old marveled as they were rolled along in foot-powered bicycle chairs, and the young, well it's none of my business what they did. The path wound along through such a tangle of vines and enormous, tropical trees that you could not see ten feet on either side, and the sun seldom, if ever, struck the ground.

But now all lovers were disgusted, for the jungle was to be cleared to make a golf course for the Everglades Club.

That spring Mr. Seth Raynor came down to lay it off. As he was considered the greatest golf architect in America, I was duly awed by his title. I don't know to this day why people want to knock a pill around a backyard, or which end of the cue to shoot with. Imagine my consternation when after ten days of a delightful visit from Mr. Raynor, I was handed a blueprint I couldn't read.

"We start here, you see, with the first tee and drive down the fairway to the second tee." His pencil skipped here and there over kidney spots and doglegs until I was bewildered and didn't know a stance from a stymie. I have never known how to spell, but I had lived opposite a Lipton electric sign in New York for years, and I knew it wasn't spelled t-e-e. So, I began to feel that we were at least brothers in spelling and, therefore, that blueprints didn't mean much more than they had to my workmen.

He left me with several big sheets of drawings and a jungle. He said he would be back to inspect the work when it was finished.

The two lasting loves of my life have always been animals and trees. Every day it was a heartbreak to see this magnificent tangle come crashing down.

All winter I had been trying to explain architectural drawings to Harold Vanderbilt, whom we called Mike. Although he could plan a yacht and its machinery, house plans were only hieroglyphics to him. Owing to the sharp dealings of one of my clients and my loss to Clarence Jones, together with picking up the pottery, I was in financial difficulties, so I sold Mike my house.[1] This left me under the sky again.

Old man Histed had some property on South County Road.[2] I finally made a dicker with him to rent the old mule shed that hadn't been used since they were building the Poinciana Hotel. I added a kitchen, pantry, baths, and divided it up into a bedroom and a huge living room, and made one end a library. By boarding it up inside and hanging tapestries and velvets on the walls, I transformed it into quite an attractive and comfortable place.[3]

I missed the new house that I sold to Mike Vanderbilt. I had killed two seven-foot rattlesnakes on the front steps and was constantly being startled by Mae shooting skunks in the sewing room. It was just as well to move.

Mae, drunk or sober, was a good cook and a social success. When one came home at night, one never knew how many people she had asked for dinner.

That year I built the John S. Phipps house and several others.[4]

I had been in Palm Beach for three years, winter and summer, and decided I needed a trip to Europe. I got myself a contractor, who had done the Munn houses the year before and had proven satisfactory. Then, he was just Lightbown, the contractor.[5]

I went to Spain and bought a half shipload of furniture and got back early in September to put the finishing touches on my houses.

In New York I heard that Wilson, my youngest brother, was dying, so I dashed over to see him. Three months before, he had been putting his car away on 59th Street just off Broadway when two men bumped into him. Evidently, a row had started, for they hit him with a church or something and broke his jaw in sixteen places. Doctors, plumbers, and linemen worked on him for hours. To keep him quiet, they fed him morphine. Wilson never did things in a small way, and at once I knew by his glassy eyes that he was full of restfulness.

He introduced me to Florence, his new companion. We decided he should be taken to Palm Beach to get out in the sunshine and recuperate.

Casa Bendita, courtyard west elevation, built for John and Margarita Grace Phipps.

I left immediately for the South, arrived, and fixed up an annex to the mule shed, and brought them down. They arrived early in the morning. I kept him riding around most of the day. Within a week he looked like a different person. Of course, I knew that that kind of hop wasn't cured in a day and only hoped he would taper off gradually.

Palm Beach was seething with local politics. They were running a man for mayor who I did not like. So, I put up Lightbown to run against him and made my first appearance as a public speaker. The town had grown enormously, for there were nearly eighty voters. I couldn't reach them all with my rallies. The day before the election I had a handbill printed saying the most terrible things about the opposing candidate in no mean terms and signed my name to each.

At sunrise, Election Day, I arrived at the polls to hand out my sweet little letters. About 7:30, Lightbown came in with his face a different vermillion from his hair, scared to death.

"The opposition candidate is outside in his car and says he is going to kill you on sight. You better get out the back way. He's in a rage."

"What's the matter with the front?"

I bolted out and grabbed the candidate by the nose and pulled it out a foot or two and let it snap back in his face.

"I heard you were looking for me?"

"Gee, you nearly broke my glasses," was all he had to say as he drove off.

All day I stood at the corner handing out my little statements. Really, I should have been shot in the gizzard, but no one interfered.

The town had declared a holiday, and groups stood around discussing me as a potbellied Yankee who was trying to run the South. Still, nothing came of it. Mae brought me my lunch in a shoe box and said she heard they were going to do something funny to the ballot boxes. When Wilson came out to go to lunch, I gave him the shoe box and told him he had better stay on the lookout. He was in his element and scowled at everyone who didn't look Lightbownish until they were afraid to vote at all.

After sundown we began the count. It looked good for my mayor. The telephone rang.

"It's Mrs. Jonas's father speaking, Mr. Jonas,[6] he says your wife is dying."

As Jonas was one of the official counters, it looked as though we would have to adjourn. Wilson jumped up and yelled, "All right, go home, but I'm staying with the ballot box!" Mr. Jonas decided to let his wife die peacefully and sat down. That hadn't worked.

A half hour later there was a shriek of "Fire! Fire!" from the grocery store next door. Everybody started for the door but Wilson and me. There was a gavel on the table. Wilson hit a leading citizen between the eyes with it as he reached in the back window for the ballot box. The meeting was again called to order, and someone spit on the fire next door. We elected Lightbown mayor.

Paris had gotten his divorce and married Joan.[7] They came down early to live in the Tibetan spasm.

He always thought I was a bit forceful about politics, but I put it down to the fact that he hadn't had a country until the war broke out. My father had been on the side of law and order in the vigilante days of early California. As he was always on the wrong side of a bet, the entire family had always coppered his judgment and been on a seesaw balanced on the borderline of the law.

Paris and Joan Singer photographed at their Chinese Villa, Peruvian Avenue.

I had a final altercation with Joe Earman about this time.[8] When I told him he ought to go and live with his aunt, I emptied the street. But, so far, I haven't been killed for my frankness.

Joe had become so unpopular that he sold the *Palm Beach Post* and was in semiretirement. The general public is too smart to take a stand against a man who has a Hell Box until someone else does. When they found that he hadn't shot me full of holes like a porous plaster, everybody took a crack at him. From his mighty heights, he became a police judge. To spite me, he had a traffic cop pinch Wilson for driving a Ford truck full of roof tiles at sixty miles an hour. At best, it couldn't make thirty, and if he had made that, the tiles would have ground up into dust.

The case came up, and Wilson was fined the limit.

"Your Honor, I wish to appeal the case."

"Why didn't you say that at first?" snapped back Earman.

"Because, if Your Honor had dismissed me, I thought I might let it go at that."

A few minutes later, Joe came down and got in his car. Wilson grabbed him by the nose. Mizners have always thought the enemy's nasal appendage was like the handle of a frying pan. It was lucky for Earman that he didn't have a hot cake on his chest, for I am sure Wilson would have flopped him over like a flapjack. But he drove away sticking out his tongue and saying, "Ah!"

That winter was very gay, and the Everglades Club was the center of everything.

Mrs. Frank P. Frazier gave a huge baby party.[9] Young and old were invited. Mr. Stotesbury went as Dr. Stork in a surgeon's smock with a huge stork painted on the front and carried a large valise filled with plumber's tools. As he was talking to old Mrs.

Green, who was so big and blonde she really looked like the eighteen-month-old baby she was dressed as, he made a pass at her. He apparently took a wriggling, little, white rabbit away from her.

The next day at lunch I asked Mrs. Green how the rabbit was.

"Oh! It's too dreadful! When I got home with it, it seemed so frightened and shivery I took it to bed with me, and this morning when I woke up, I couldn't find it anywhere."

There was a terrible hush. Everyone was afraid to guess where it had gone.

Paris always loved pageants and parties, why, I never understood. For although his costumes were always wonderfully done, he never seemed to enter into the gaiety but stood in the background looking on. He was always dreaming of how he could do something else to make Palm Beach more attractive. I am sure this was never out of his mind.

John Harris, Ed Shearson, Ned Stotesbury, and Bill Warden, with others, were constantly complaining that all the golf courses were too crowded and were talking of organizing a new club. I began snooping around and finally doped out a scheme that combined everything.

Four miles south, the ridge was only five hundred feet wide between ocean and lake. Paris and I talked over a lovely clubhouse on this high elevation. There would be swimming cradles to bring the fishing boats up on the beach, tennis courts, and the like. At the back, there would be broad staircases through lovely radiant gardens leading to a landing on the lake. Little speed boats could snap across the lake in three minutes, where property was ideal and absurdly cheap.

I called a meeting and showed them all the land and a rough layout of what we knew could be done. I had a week's option on the land. Everyone at the meeting had a different objection, agreeing on only one subject: It was too far away. As they left, saying they would think it over, I made one request, "Don't tell anyone about it, least of all anyone in the real estate business."

Within an hour, they each had their real estate broker under their arm and were rushing frantically around boosting the price of property. Each wanted the first tee—I had learned that Lipton was wrong by now—right under their own bed. This started further arguments. Inside a week, you couldn't get five acres together for less than a king's ransom within a radius of miles.

Paris, with his usual foresight, had gone down the coast fifteen miles and bought several hundred acres below Boynton. He waited for the serious businessmen to find that there was nothing to be had, since they had let options run out and could get nothing. Then, he offered them his property at cost. They finally took it over and organized the Gulf Stream Golf Club.

I defy a drunk to pronounce it. Perhaps they didn't want those dries who had tried to get wet there.

It was the end of the season when a committee rushed in and wanted plans. In six hours, I turned over plans and sketches, which they quickly approved. Specifications and details were rushed through, and Lightbown got the contract.

For months, I had been talking house with the William Wardens.[10] Mrs. Warden wanted a nice, comfortable, big house. Bill wanted something small, as he hated ostentation, something that would not overshadow the houses next to his. They had a block on the North Ocean Boulevard. Across the street was a small clapboard house, and in the other direction, a stucco house.

I took up my sketchbook and drew in these two houses in a large and important manner. Then, I went back to the office and designed the Warden house one-half the scale of the others. It looked rather long, but truly insignificant. As I had told Mrs. Warden the trick, everybody was satisfied.

By the middle of April, Bill went home with his two floor plans under his arm. The contract was let, and work was started.

In the first part of October, I got a telegram from him saying he was coming down. I was scared to death. The building ran the whole length of the block and a couple of hundred feet down the side street. It was designed to get the privacy of a huge, central patio. In fear and trembling, I met him at the station with a constant stream of chattiness. We walked through the building, and he seemed rather pleased.

"This gives a really big garden, doesn't it?" he said, as he viewed the court.

As he was to leave the next night, I never left his side and stepped with all my might on the charm pedal. Just before train time, we took a last look about.

"By the way, Addison, you have never sent me any elevations of the house. I have nothing but the floor plans, and a couple of architect friends of mine want to see what I am doing down here."

"Elevations! Why Bill, you look intelligent at times. How could I send you elevations when the house isn't finished yet?"

He looked a little bewildered, even befuddled, and wasn't sure what a stalling summer squash I was until he told his professional friends about it.

Thank God, I haven't seen my own elevations since I passed the two hundred fifty-pound mark.

7

Things were moving too fast to get tangled up. In 1921, I had built a house for myself nearer town than the Vanderbilt house, lived in it for a winter, and sold it to Mrs. Sloane.[1] I was getting to be a transient. So, I went five miles further down, bought three hundred feet, and built. Surely, no one would want this one.[2] But I was wrong. During the second year that I owned Sin Cuidado, I sold it to Edward Moore. Then, I built an apartment for myself next to my office and opposite the entrance of the Everglades Club.[3] This was the start of the Via Mizner.

Concha Marina, 102 Jungle Road. Mizner's second residence that he sold to Isabel Dodge Sloane, pictured above with her niece by the saltwater swimming pool.

Sin Cuidado, 1800 South Ocean Boulevard. Original facade, east elevation. Addison Mizner's third residence that he sold to Edward S. Moore, whose brother Paul Moore built Collado Hueco, the Mizner-designed house directly to the south at 1820 South Ocean Boulevard.

Since 1919, I had passed on an average of $5 million each year through the West Palm Beach banks, and that sister town across the lake was growing in leaps and bounds. All the money I could gather in from any resources that I had outside of the state, I had reinvested in or about Palm Beach. Paris and I were beginning to see the dawn of our dreams coming true. Truly, Palm Beach was blossoming into the winter capital of the world and had proven Mr. Singer a true prophet.

Mr. Wead should also come in for a share of our optimism. For every day he would say, "It's going to be the biggest season we ever had, nine thousand or nine million people will be here this winter." The numeral nine was his favorite, and it didn't make any difference to him how many zeros you put behind it.[4]

The follow-up was the hardest part of my work. For no matter who you told to do a thing, you had to see that they did it. Mr. Wead was the only exception. No matter what you told him to do, he did it. When they were clearing the jungle, a couple of men got a rope around the neck of a six-foot rattlesnake and brought him in alive for the alligator farm. As they pulled him out of the trunk, I told Mr. Wead to pick him up and bring him to me. The old man shuffled after it and had to be stopped forcibly by the men. He was very indignant when I told him to stop.

There was a little garden around the office, and we had a week of dry weather. "Mr. Wead, will you water the garden every afternoon at four thirty? Don't forget, no matter what happens."

A few days later there was a terrific thunderstorm, and the rain came down in sheets. I stepped out onto the porch to watch the deluge, and there under an umbrella was Mr. Wead plying the hose.

I had started a lot of young fellows in business, and there was only one who didn't hate me for it. Before I came to Florida, I was building a colonial house at Roslyn, and my rather fussy client was trying to match the walls to an old gray fireplace.[5] There was a young man with China-blue eyes who was very patient and mixed shade after shade with so much diplomacy and goodwill that he stuck in my mind.

When I was starting the Everglades Club, he showed up and asked for a job. I made him head painter. One day I told him to mix a dipper full of cobalt blue powder with one-half a dipper full of chrome green and three of plain whitewash and do the cornice.

"Don't you mean oil colors?"

"No! Watercolors; I don't want oil. It's too shiny."

I had to be gone for several hours, and when I came back, I found fifty feet of cornice glistening in the sun. You had to put smoked glasses on to look at it. I jumped up and down, threw a fit, and fired him on the spot. As he gathered up his tools, I could hear him mumbling, "The poor sap ought to know that you have to preserve outside woodwork with oil."

I didn't bother to tell him that you didn't have to preserve pecky cypress with anything.

A year later, he came to tell me that he had thought me crazy, but now that the club was finished, it looked pretty good. I took him back. Today, Dayton Kort is the best antiquer and mural man I know, and the old good and faithful friend of the fifty I put on their feet.

One afternoon I was inspecting the plumbing at the club when I heard the sounds of battle coming from one of the cottages. I tore over to see what the matter was. There was a big, ugly guy who had all the rest terrified and had appointed himself leader. A little Cracker carpenter was tearing into two others with a hatchet, and as they were all working on a roof, it looked precarious. Two of them jumped off and broke a new tree that I had just moved in. The Cracker and two friends started down the ladder just as the big guy picked up a huge monkey wrench and started for the bottom of the ladder, calling for his cohorts to follow.

By this time, it was like a war with Turkey. Everybody wanted to get into it, running from every direction. It was war, and I didn't have long to decide. I took a running kick at the big guy. When I got my foot out, I pulled the ladder out from under the others, which stunned them to no end.

I have heard since that my extemporaneous speech was a masterpiece, the diction clear, and the billingsgate was fluid. That was that, and I never had any more trouble of that sort.

After several years had gone by, everything was turned over to contractors. This gave me time to travel again.

I had met the Joshua Cosdens in 1920.[6] They had rented houses for several years when Nell got the building bee. They

Playa Riente, aerial view looking west toward Lake Worth.

bought the only piece of property on the North Ocean Boulevard that did not have a road between it and the ocean.[7] When she spoke to me about building there, I was thrilled.

I spent all night working on an old Gothic palace built out into the sea, with a great Gothic hallway framing a vista from the front door straight through to the ocean. A stairway led up to the main floor, which was to occupy the top of the ridge.

The house has never been changed from those original sketches. The one thing I am proud of is the engineering. Although the great September storms beat against foundations and the waves dash forty feet up its sides, they have never had five cents worth of damage.

Nell was so lovely to look at that I thought she must be dumb. She had never seen a blueprint in her life, but within three weeks she could read a plan better than I could, even to the plumbing chases and the electric conduits.

With all my houses I had made a stipulation that I must be consulted about the first-floor furnishings. I didn't care what people did in their bedrooms, you know, about the furnishings, but I was adamant about having things in keeping.

One day, when the foundations were in, Nell said, "I hear you are going to Spain. Let Josh and me go with you, and we can get the furniture."

At the last minute, Mr. Cosden couldn't go. Nell asked the most beautiful and attractive girl to go as a sort of chaperone.

The night before we sailed, I met a man I knew slightly as I was going into the Ritz to have a lonely dinner. I asked him to join me. As we were finishing dinner, he asked me what I was doing later. He said some girlfriends were giving a little party and would I like to go.

We strolled up Park Avenue and were taken to a beautiful apartment. Every year it was getting harder to tell the fruit from the flowers, and to this day I don't know which box I was in. There were about twelve or fifteen others there, and everything was refinement itself. After about ten minutes, one of the girls went to a cabinet and took out a white folded paper and a nail file. She started passing it around. As everybody took a sniff, I didn't want to be rude. When it came to me, I imitated the rest. The result was almost instantaneous. I wanted to carry the grand piano around and talk. Everyone began talking at once. No one seemed to care whether anyone was listening.

Again and again, the paper went around. The old world seemed to be a drab and distant thing. Gaiety was flamboyant. The world ahead was like a golden sunrise, full of promises that were sure to be fulfilled. I looked at my watch. It was eight o'clock and thin lines of light were filtering in through the drawn curtains. There was no sense of disorder, just gaiety and conversation. No tables were overturned. No sots asleep on the floor. Even the ashtrays had been emptied. There was no clutter of dirty glasses, just pure and orderly joy.

With an effort, I thought of unpacked luggage and a steamer that sailed on the tide at ten o'clock.[8] I got back to the hotel, helped the valet pack things up, and made the boat in plenty of time.

Nell introduced me to Peg.[9] Her hair was so *bien soigné*. Her straight, slender figure was almost boyish. Her great, dark eyes sparkled, in no mean way, out of a face that was brilliant with color and had no makeup. It couldn't be true. It must be the cocaine. I shook my head, but she looked just the same, even better. Then, there was the big kitchen laugh that made you join in as she greeted some old friends.

I took a walk around the ship, came back, and looked again. She hadn't changed a bit, but my nerves had. They were beginning to go to pieces. The hum of the machinery had started, and I almost jumped out of my skin. I didn't want to see anybody, but I was afraid to be alone. Gawd! It was awful!

I went to my cabin, thinking I needed sleep, but found that was the last thing I wanted. My legs were tired and sank into a deck chair next to Peggy.

"Are you always as nervous as this?" she said.

I gave her a quick look.

"Never had a nerve in my body before."

"What's the matter? Were you in your cups last night? That's the way my brothers jump after they have been dipping the beak."

I had to tell somebody, and I fessed up. I thought I might as well put her out of my life right now, and kept thinking, *You old fool. She can't be more than twenty-two or three, and you're nearly fifty.*

Do you think she was shocked? No. She pooled herself right onto the edge of the chair and wanted to know all the details. She was delighted. "What can you take to make you feel better?"

"There is nothing, I guess, but a shot of morphine or a dive overboard, and I'm not going to try either. If I live, I'm through, but it was grand while it lasted."

For two days, I was fit to be tied. I can't see how anybody can go up against the stuff a second time. I was through with the snow. Whoever wants to go skiing can, but no more sleighing for me.

We landed at Cherbourg. Charlie Munn had sent his Rolls to meet us, and we started on our way to Paris. Mile after mile, and hour after hour, we sped on. Every five kilometers we would pass a sign, "So many miles to Vittel, Europe's greatest watering place." I was ready to blow up in their faces and began to wriggle. Then I thought of the next six weeks of motoring in Spain. If they were camels, I wasn't.

"I don't care where, but the next boy's fainting room we see, I faint."

So, we came to an understanding right then and there.

I picked up Alex Waugh in Paris, who was to act as my checker, et cetera.[10] We left the girls in Paris to start dressmaking, while we went on to Spain to get the ball rolling. I promised to come back to Burgos and meet them ten days later.

The train arrived at Salamanca on Sunday morning at four thirty. A cold wind chilled us to the marrow, and a rickety, rattly, old bus met us. The hotel smelt like all the shoestrings in the world and was horrible.

Everywhere huge bullfight posters blazed forth, but I was too disgusted to look at them. Waugh kept looking longingly at them and half a dozen times told me the fight was today. I had seen hundreds of corridas and was in a bad humor because the shops weren't open. All my old friends seemed to be so busy, as "They would see me after the bullfight." I broke down and told the porter to get me two of the best seats. After an hour or so he came back beaming: two seats had been turned back. The price was several times what it should have been, but I was too tired to argue.

We went sightseeing and stopped late at an open-air restaurant where rancid olive oil cooking smelt less horrible than at the hotel. We lingered long over our sherry.

I hadn't yet read the announcement attached to the posters when we decided to walk to the bullring. Spain is the one country in Europe where its smaller cities are just like they were five hundred years ago. We were crossing a small plaza surrounded by Gothic and Romanesque palaces when I heard a fanfare of trumpets. Two prancing horses came out of a narrow street at the far end with gorgeously costumed trumpeters whose long horns had embroidered hanging banners. Close behind them came the king with his jeweled crown fixed to his steel helmet.

The king was followed by three hundred men in armor carrying lances. The emblazoned trappings of their horses dragged nearly to the ground, while the splendid feathers on the horses' head armor blew in the breeze. Trundling at the back came a dozen lumbering oxcarts with the queen in her Gothic robes of state surrounded by her court of ladies-in-waiting, pages, and servants. Every costume was real and of the period, as was the armor. Musty old chests had been taken out of attics and produced this splendor all over again after centuries of Rip Van Winkle.

For a minute I thought it must be the sherry, but Waugh said he had seen it, too. The procession took the little street at the corner and was gone. It took me minutes to come to, and then we hurried to the ring. If the pageant had startled me, it hadn't warned me of what was yet to come.

The entire arena was hung in old velvets, tapestries, and embroideries. The king had dismounted and was leading the queen to her bower. All the audience were in costume. Even on the sunny side of the ring, the peasants had gotten out their finery. What a haul for an antiquary was exhibited that day.

Tilting matches started at once. Even when a neighbor sneeringly told me that the horsemen who took the parts of contenders were cavalrymen whose lances were sawed one-half through and that he had no hope of seeing anyone killed, it still seemed that I was living in the fifteenth century.

It wasn't until I got back to the hotel, where some of my old classmates[11] joined me, that I found out it was only a show put on for the Red Cross in Morocco. They had gathered up things from all over Spain, even from the museums, to costume it. It still lives with me as a real peek into the Dark Ages.

From Salamanca, we went on to Avila—that wonderful old city with its walls just as they stood eight hundred years ago. The hotel was better. We made a pilgrimage to Santo Tomas to see the tomb of Prince John, the nineteen-year-old, only son of Ferdinand and Isabella—the end of the houses of Castile and Aragon, where every grandee still says a prayer to the old dynasty in semi-disloyalty to the newer Hapsburgs.

I'm sorry. I didn't mean to get so travelogue. I must sound like Burton Holmes.[12]

We were stuck in Avila. There was only one car to hire, and that was the hotel bus, a brand-new Ford chassis on which they had set the much too heavy body of the old horse stage. I had bought a lot of junk, and there was little room for us as we trundled toward Madrid.

Oh, my gawd, what a trip! We had to cross a ridge of mountains. Every few miles the teapot boiled over, and we had to wait until she lost her passion and got her breath. The damned thing rattled and settled right down on her springs. I was dead with a headache, and no one had ever heard of Mr. Emerson or knew what drink had made Ballymore famous.[13]

When we got to the Madrid Ritz, I was white with dirt and sweat and tangled up with antique furniture. The doorman didn't know whether to use a spade or obstetrics to get me out. In fact, he didn't want me to get out at all.

It was like the time I went to Newport to visit Mrs. Belmont. I got off the boat in my new suit, looking my very cutest, and chartered the surrey with the longest fringe on its umbrella top, and just said, "Marble House." We clattered up Bellevue Avenue at a smart pace, and I leaned back, thinking how nice it was to be one of this effete colony. When we got within a block of my destination, the driver turned in his seat and said, "Front or back?"

And that was the look this magnificent concierge gave me now. But they finally removed me without sending the bus to the women's hospital. I made it to my room and bathtub when there was a rap at the door, and the page handed me a pasteboard that stated, "The American Ambassador."

How clever of Alexander Moore to leave a deck of them in the office and have one left on each American arrival,[14] I thought, as I gulped down an overdose of Bromo Seltzer.

I hopped into my tub and was just getting the first rapports from the blue bottle when there was another bang on the door.

"Come in!" I yelled, immodestly, and the door opened. Jimmy Walker in his heyday never looked like that.[15] Shiny silk hat and white spats. It was perfect.

I couldn't pull a Lady Godiva, so I started to make suds, as the apparition came directly into the bathroom and took the only seat available.

"That's a hell of a way to treat your ambassador. Keep him waiting in the hall while you soak your big hips."

We understood one another at once. Lillian Russell[16] had been Mrs. Moore and died just before Alex came to Spain. She had been a great friend of mine, so we started right from there.

Alex had done more to make good relations between Spain and America than all the dubs before him put together and all the saps that might follow. I knew most of the court and knew how wonderfully he stood with the royal family and down to the poorest peasant. I asked him how he did it.

"Oh, I just thought of the brickyard back in Pittsburgh and knew I wasn't cut out to be la-di-da and a cotton-back imitation of the king. So, I just sold them plain Alex Moore, and it has gone over fine."

I'm thinking of another ambassador whose wife said, "I saw you at the king's races yesterday. You were with the very smartest people in Spain—all of the court set. How did you get to know them?"

"Just born that way, I guess," I said, naively.

"Do you speak Spanish? You do! It doesn't really matter here though, does it, for everyone speaks such beautiful English. I don't mean American."

At the end of the week, I took the night train back to Burgos to meet the girls. My heart sank when I saw their glistening Rolls-Royce draw up in front of the hotel. That would boost prices.

We took in the sights all day and turned in early. It was great. Peggy was more intriguing than ever, so vital and interested. I went to bed calling myself an old fool and trying to think that my dogs and monkey at home were companions enough.

The hotel was next to the police station and across the street from the barracks. Just before dawn, bugles blew, and horses stamped. Being a very early riser, I got up and went downstairs. It was one of those brittle, cold mornings in early June that one finds in the mountains. I peeked into the bleak icebox they called the dining room, ordered my coffee, and began seeking a warm spot to have it in.

Finally, I discovered the first rays of the sun peeking in the bay window at the end of the great salon. Several men with carpet tied on their feet were skating about, polishing the oak floor.

I beckoned the waiter and told him to fetch my coffee into the sunshine. He told me in a very ugly way that was what the dining room was for and refused. I went back to the dining room and brought it out myself. By this time, he was in a rage.

For fear some of you do not understand what assault means in a Latin country, let me explain. If you commit just a simple murder, the police wait on you. But, for a punch in the nose, you wait on them, and indefinitely, try to get a hearing. The waiter pranced about me, doing a sort of an Indian incantation, saying dreadful things, and threatening me with Hell's fires. I sipped my coffee in silence with a beatific smile, as if he were a songbird enjoying the first warm rays with me.

Finally, he had whipped up his passion to such a state that he stuck his face in mine so that I could see as well as hear. This was unpleasant, for his voice with fetid with garlic. Then we both made our mistake. He tried to snatch my tray, and I socked him. He scudded away across the glassy floor, tripping up the skaters as he went and piling up furniture in odd piles. In an instant, the place was a shambles. Shrieks and screams were coming from every direction. The uninjured man crawled out on his hands and knees, shouting for the police, the military, and even for the minister of war. Instantly, the place was flooded with uniforms. I had never seen so much gold braid and so many different ranks together in my life. Even the firemen responded to the call.

It was serious. Everyone was talking at once, and the accusing waiter was the most active. Finally, I picked out the man with the most lace on him and slipped him a hard, round American silver dollar. Instantly, he cleared the room.

I woke the girls, sent up their breakfast, and ordered a retreat. They couldn't make out just what was the matter but obeyed without a word. For you see, they were in my power.

They did not know a word of Spanish and couldn't even powder their noses without asking me.

Within the hour, we were sliding out over the fields of poppies. I breathed more freely as the lacy lantern and spires of the cathedral sank behind a hill.

In Madrid, Nell's maid, Louise, had the rooms in order and the trunks unpacked. We had tea in the sitting room, a siesta, and observed the old Spanish custom of dining in the garden at eleven thirty.

We dined with the Duke de Alba, lunched with the Marquis de Villa Viejo, and so on. But, for the most part, we were skimming the scum of back alleys and thieves' markets for goodies. Nell learned in no time to judge furniture and could smell out the slightest restoration in an old piece.

Sunday came, and Louise had been coaxing me to get Nell to let her see a bullfight. As we all had a box, I convinced Nell to take Louise along as the dueña. Louise, lugging a huge camera, brought up the tail end of the procession. I bought huge fans for the girls to hide behind when the horses were being disemboweled. I had to watch all the time so as to tell them when not to look. Louise was clicking her camera from behind on a higher tier of seats. "Don't look!" It was a little more horrible than usual as the bull tore a horse into ribbons. Suddenly, there was a dull, sickening thud from behind, followed by a loud pop. Louise had fainted and fallen off her seat with her camera.

I thought I was hiding my gooey state over Peggy splendidly, by kidding and quipping, but Nell was on. Peggy was a wicked little devil and teased me to death.

"When I marry, I want a lot of children."

I was nearly fifty and told her we had better hurry up, as I was fast running out of them. The days sped on as I got mushier and mushier and tried more and more to turn it into a joke.

Down through Seville, Granada, and dozens of small towns, we laughed our way through the happiest two months of my life. When they dumped me off on a street corner in Nice, tears were standing in my eyes. They were going on to Florence to see the work the Angeli brothers had done in restoring the frescoes in the Davanzati Palace,[17] while I was stopping off to visit the Singers at Cap Ferrat. It was a terrible parting. I arrived just in time for the Singers' annual fight.

8

I had been away from Paris for two months without mail, so I telegraphed Morgan & Company to send it down.

The row at the Singers was the usual one. Paris had been naughty and promptly started the battle to throw the onus on poor Joan. As usual, I became the telephone. Tart and stinging remarks were all made to me as if the other person were not in the room. I was sick and tired, for the bad food always stirred up my old tripe trouble. And besides, I was unhappy at my parting from Peggy.

The mail came. The first thing I opened was a blue cablegram from San Francisco, which had been laying in Paris for six weeks. My only sister, Min, had died on the other side of the globe, and I had not known it all this time. True, I hadn't seen her for eighteen years, but still, it added much to the gloom.

The "Many Mizners" were beginning to cool off at about the rate of one every two years.[1] Lansing had snapped off four years ago. Edgar died two years back, and now, Min. The Mizners were rapidly getting into the short division class, although there wasn't such a much to divide.

I spent ten days of Hell. Paris would sneak off to bed at eight o'clock and couldn't sleep after two.[2] He would come in to tell me something new he had thought up about Joan. What a good slapping in his youth would have done for him!

Had Joan fought him back, just torn into him right from the first, everything would have been over in a moment. She just sat frozen-faced and tight-lipped, locking herself in her room when things got too hot. This infuriated Paris more than he could bear.

He loved a fight and really adored Joan. The more he knew that he was in the wrong, the madder he would get.

I did some sketches and made some suggestions on and for the magnificent, great, medieval villa he was building and left singing hallelujah.

I was to meet Jose Marie Sert in Venice and see the sketches he had made for the Cosden ballroom.[3] We had already signed the contract, and I only had to approve the proof.

Henry, my clergyman brother, better known in our outlaw family as the blot on the escutcheon, was to meet me there also, with his wife and his little girl, Alice. I had a wonderful time showing him *my* Venice.

Sert's sketches were lovely beyond any dream, and as I had stopped off in Florence to sign up the Angelis to do the dining room and loggia, I was happy to be idle for a couple of weeks.

I am so bad at remembering dates, but I think this was the year of the first Fascista uprising. Anyway, it was one year when for the first time I heard the name even as a myth. No one seemed to think it was a serious thing.

The band was playing in the piazzetta, and the usual crowd was milling around. All the tables at Florian's were taken. Suddenly, at the far end and opposite San Marco, we heard the faint wail of a fife and the rattle of drums. Then came pouring through the arches a disorderly crowd of boys singing a song. They stopped near the bandstand and hoisted one of their lads on their shoulders. He began making a harangue.

Instantly, the police burst out of their station, located next to Florian's, arrested the speaker, and dragged him into their quarters. It was like vanishing cream. The piazzetta was cleared in a twinkle, leaving nothing but the Fascisti, the police, and me. The kids rushed to the police station, took back their speaker, and went on with the march through the arch of the clock tower and up the Mercado to the Rialto. The next day, papers were full of it. As far as I know, this was their first demonstration in all of Italy. In the entire mob, I did not see a lad who looked eighteen.

My holiday was over. I had no more excuse for staying away from work, and I sailed home.

Peggy was terribly nice to me in New York. I was filled with delight and terror when she told me she was coming to Palm Beach to take charge of Mrs. Franklin's Shop. It was quite the chic thing now for girls of the very best families who didn't have a lot of money to do this sort of thing. Everywhere you turned, you ran into a grand duchess selling drawers or a prince selling caviar.

The Via Mizner was finished.[4] Mrs. Franklin had taken number eleven. George Lamaze had number four as El Patio Restaurant. Most of the ultras were in Mizner's Alley. Palm Beach was rapidly coming up to our dreams.

But I'm ahead of myself. When I was living in the house way down the Ocean Boulevard, a couple of years ago, I first heard of the Searles. "Whispering" Quinn came in to tell me he might have a prospect for me.[5] The story was like this:

The day before, a highly varnished limousine had stopped in front of his office, and the chauffeur came in to ask Mr. Quinn if he could come out, as the *lady* was so heavy it took a lot of squeezing and shoving to get her out of the car. They said they wanted to look at houses, so Quinn climbed into the backseat with Mr. Searles, and they were off. The first house they stopped at Mrs. Searles said, "Go inside, Victor, and see what you think of it." A few minutes later Victor returned and said, "Fine."

"How much is it, Mr. Quinn?" queried Mrs. Searles.

"Only $50,000? Well, we'll take it."

She reached down in the front of her dress, pulled out a wad that would choke a boa constrictor, and peeled off fifty $1,000 bills.

"Wait a minute," said Quinn. "You can't pay me until you see the title."

She hadn't stirred from her seat.

The next day they came again and said although they would take the house, they would keep it just as an investment. They wanted to see something on the Ocean Drive, as an acquaintance at the hotel told them that it was sweller. They bought the property next to mine, which had a square Cracker box atrocity on it. Mrs. Searles said she wanted to dress it up a bit, and Quinn suggested that I call. So, I left my name and asked them to dinner the following night.

Quinn asked me who they could be. With my indexed mind, I found a cell that held the story.

When Mark Hopkins had built his palace on Nob Hill in San Francisco, he had given a huge contract to Herter Brothers of New York for the interiors. They had sent out a very gaudy and good-looking young man of about twenty-five to carry out the work. Before its completion, the old man took a one-way ticket to heaven. He left a sorrowing young widow of seventy-six summers to marry the beautiful gallant, take him out of the sloughs of the decorating business, and set him up in an older profession. Within a couple of years, she joined her unlamented, and young Searles inherited sixty or seventy million.

That was nearly fifty years ago. Now the young man turned gray and doddering, had joined his bride, and left his accumulated millions to a clerk living in one room in Brooklyn. Somewhere, somehow, a nephew had turned up and settled for seven or eight million in cash—Victor must be the nephew.[6]

Although Mr. Quinn had warned me that they were peculiar, I was in no way prepared for my dinner guests. Promptly at seven thirty they arrived. As one opened my front door, there was a hall with two dressing rooms, then, a short flight of easy stairs to the loggia that looked out to the ocean on one side and the lake on the other. There I waited to receive my guests, thinking what a hit it would make with them when they saw that they could get two views at once.

But I was wrong. My brother Wilson and their chauffeur hauled, shoved, and dragged something into the doorway, the like of which I had never seen before. She had enough breath to gasp, "Why in hell do you have a chicken ladder a mile long before you get into this lousy place? Gee, I'm all wore out." All the chairs had arms, and I saw instantly that she couldn't jam into any of them, so I dragged out an armless one from the next room, which she backed up to. She must have had fishhooks on the seat of her pants, for only one-third of her could get on the seat, but she stuck.

The chauffeur had gone back for another load and again appeared with a companion piece that was unequalled in any museum in the world. "That's Victor," she said, pointing her thumb over her shoulder, and it was. Rocking and bleary-eyed, with big whiskey blotches all over his face, he stood for a minute and fell in a heap.

Hilda, the pretty little eighteen-year-old maid, had to step over him to serve the hors d'oeuvres. The chauffeur and the butler got him onto the sofa before Mr. and Mrs. Quinn arrived. The crash sort of brightened him up, for as Hilda passed him the tray, he grabbed her hand in one of his, while with the other he started running up and down her arm. I thought he was whetting a razor, but Mrs. Searles said, "No, he is just getting fresh."

How we ever got through that dinner I will never know, with Wilson yelling, "Stop that, you old rat!" and Hilda trying to serve him without losing all her clothes. But finally, we made it to the living room, where he spread himself out on the sofa and began snoring loudly. She wheezed over to him, put a pillow under his head, slapped his mouth shut, and settled down for a long winter's night.

"I never take that drunken old sot out in refined company that he doesn't disgrace me. 'Specially, just as I got to know you folks and like you. Let him alone, and he'll sleep it off.

"I'll never forget the first night I ever saw him," she said, as she glanced at Victor. "He was lying in the gutter outside Dirty Dan's in Boston. You know, down on the waterfront? It was about five in the morning, and me and another girl stepped out into the street to get a little air, and there he was, just as though he was dead. But I knew right away, he wasn't. I knew he was just drunk. You see, at Dan's we get a lot of those to handle, so I called a stevedore friend of mine, and we got him up to my room and threw him on the floor. The girls all say I'm too good-hearted, but you can't let a bum get pinched just for sleeping. Well, the next afternoon, I poured half a bottle of whiskey down him but wouldn't let him get drunk no more.

"He told me his name was Searles and that he was a nephew of the guy that had just died and left all those millions. Of course, I didn't believe him at first 'cause the papers said the old man didn't have any relations. But after I had asked him a lot of questions, I began to be suspicious he was on the level. I made him stay right there until I did some sleuthing.

"The next day I thought it was a good bet for a plunge of seventy-five bucks. I gave him a bath, bought him a hand-me-down, even to socks and new shoes, and took him around to Mr. Whipple, you know, the biggest fellow in his racket in Boston. He asked a lot more questions and then sent out some scouts to see if the old souse was on the square. Pretty soon they came running back, all out of breath and excited. They told Mr. Whipple the old sot was on the square. So, he took the case, and here we are."

The old girl couldn't have been more than five feet and two inches standing up and surely not more than five feet and six inches lying down. But she was full, every quart of her, of purpose and determination.

"Two months ago, we got the dough right in the lily white. I say 'we,' because that was the arrangement. As soon as the judge got through marrying us, I slipped a fountain pen in his mitt and said, "Sign there," and he split even with his Peerless Irene; that's what he calls me."

She was just a babble of conversation.

"Say, I noticed you didn't have a lace tablecloth. Ain't that stylish anymore?"

I knew she wouldn't know about the patina on a fifteenth-century table, so I merely said, "Oh, for ladies, but you see I'm a bachelor and have to have the washing done out," and let it go at that.

"We went to Atlantic City for our honeymoon. I bought a beautiful tablecloth and a lot of things, and some fellows are coming to unpack tomorrow. Then you have got to come and have dinner with us. How about Tuesday night?

"Say, you're sort of heavy yourself. Why don't you do like me? I had eighteen inches of stuff cut off my stomach only a little while ago. The doctor said it wasn't anything. Said it was just lard. He took it out with a spoon."

Wilson shook Victor violently and brought him to. He had four hours of sleep and was able to get out under his own power, but it took us both to get Irene down to her car and the aid of the chauffeur to tuck her in.

When we got the return dinner, Victor wasn't quite so drunk and ushered us into the parlor. As soon as we were seated, he kicked a big brass spittoon up to each of us and offered us each a big black cigar. The room was wonderful. Dozens of marble statues and bronze lamps, all naked except for the lamp shades.

He didn't know about cocktails. A slovenly, old wench brought in a bottle of whiskey and a stack of glasses.

"Missouri don't look like much, but it's safer with that old letch," said Irene.

We went in to dinner. There was a point lace tablecloth that had cost well over a thousand, a $16 set of dishes, and ham and eggs. Everything looked like an auctioneer's window on the boardwalk, and they were as pleased as a clam at high tide.

I got to sort of like Peerless Irene, for at least she wasn't pretending much.

They bought a mile of oceanfront at Boynton and a lot of acreage. She had a good business head. Things would have been all right if a year later she hadn't dozed off one night and smothered to death.

Victor was beside himself. He ordered a $9,000 cast-bronze casket, with a three-fourths-inch plate-glass top. It took all the piano movers in town to lift it empty, and when they got Irene full of embalming fluid in it, I don't know how they ever got it into Ferguson's Funeral Parlor.

The second day after the demise, Victor came in draped in crepe.

"That was the greatest woman that ever lived, and I want to put her away right. I saw a picture of the Taj Mahal once, and I want you to copy it for me, so she'll have a swell home."

I had listened to so many of his dreams that I didn't lose any sleep working on the plans. Several days later I met him on a street corner in West Palm Beach and stopped to talk to him. A fellow came up and said he was glad to see Victor looking so well. He said he had just got back from a trip. We were introduced.

"Where is Irene?" he asked.

"Just across the street. Would you like to see her?"

He pointed to Ferguson's Funeral Parlor. It didn't seem to register with the stranger, so I followed on behind. We stepped into a business office and through into a back room. The man looked a little befuddled as Victor slid back the lid, and then the man almost fainted. He hadn't heard that the great spirit of the Peerless Irene had passed on.

The Taj Mahal was never copied, for three weeks of widowhood was enough. He took the chauffeur's girl away from him and married her.

The last reports I have are that his erstwhile cook is suing him for parentage. He is hiding from processors. His wife is getting a divorce. Irene is still at Ferguson's, as just a rumor, and hasn't gotten a home. So, someday if West Palm Beach hears a loud explosion, it's a ten to one shot, it's Irene.

9

All general intimacy in the Mizner family had broken up in 1888 when my father accepted the American minister's portfolio to the five countries of Central America.[1] Mother had tried to hold us together with postage stamps. But at her death in 1915, all the mucilage melted, and we became myths in one another's lives. Wilson and I had kept more or less in touch, at least through the newspapers. Otherwise, thousands of miles separated me from the others.

Now that Horace Chase Jr. was with me, I was delighted to hear from him that his sister Ysabel wanted to come down and see him. I had last seen her in New York when she was going to school there. Although she signed herself "America's Foremost Beauty," "Venus de Milo," or "Lola Montague," she knew this was an exaggeration. She said that when she looked in a mirror, she looked so much like a llama that she was expecting any minute to be spit at, like they do in the zoo. A more accurate picture of Ysabel is the first illustration of Alice in *The Looking Glass*. She has blonde, straight hair; had a lovely, slender figure; and was, and still is, the funniest woman I have ever known. At first glance, you would think she was a lady, but she wasn't. She was just a Mizner.

We can sit by the hour and laugh and gab. She is the only human being in the world with whom I would be willing to be shipwrecked on a desert island and stands out as the only person who can put Wilson in his place.

I will never forget one day when the boom was on, and my office door flew open during a conference. A strange and awful face appeared.

"Hello, Cousin Addison. I'm your cousin Edgar Cairns."

"How do you do, sir? I'm very busy just now. Won't you come back and have lunch with me at one?"

"That will be fine. I'll bring my wife and twenty-one month-old baby, too."

I had never heard of him before in my life but knew, vaguely, that his last name was somewhere in the outer branches of the family jungle.

They arrived. Cousin Mae was even worse than Cousin Edgar. But the child—my heavens! We sat down at the refectory table, which was my prize possession. The baby took the old silver service plate in her two dear little chubby hands, turned it on edge, and started gouging the strips of inlay out of the board. Her mother took the plate away from her and said, "Baby, dear, mustn't do that. She might hurt herself."

She never knew how near she was to getting hurt. She took a butter ball and stuck it in her mouth. And not liking it, she spit it across the table onto my plate. All the time, Cousin Edgar was keeping up a running conversation that no poultice could bring to a head. He never forgot to say "Cousin Addison" every two minutes. I looked at Ysabel. Her mouth was a tight line. She was holding onto the chair seat with both hands and controlling herself.

We struggled through the meal and went into the living room. On the taboret next to my chair was a fourteenth-century Moorish luster bowl filled with matches. The darling little thing picked this up and dashed it on the tile floor.

Cousin Edgar hadn't addressed a word to my lovely niece before, but now turned to her.

"Isn't she cute, Cousin Ysabel?"

"You're no relation of mine. I'm illegitimate," and went on with her tapestry work. Needless to say, I have never heard from my cousins since.

No Mizner has ever had to think what to say in a crisis. It was trying not to say it that came hard.

Flo Ziegfeld would never have picked Ysabel out of a crowd. She had more between the ears than all the choruses I ever saw him put together. She had "IT," with suitors all over the place. She was really quite pretty when a new beau would turn up. She would have her hair curled and use a lipstick. Sometimes this would last two or three days. Then, just as she looked her best and had on a new gown, she would decide whether the dogs should be washed or the bougainvillea trimmed.

You couldn't send her to the dressmaker. When I did drag her to one, it was always enough to throw a shop into a panic. She could make the smartest gown in the world look as though comic actress Marie Dressler had made it. For one instant, it would be a slapstick comedy, and the next, a tragedy.

In her childhood, she had been brought up in the lap of luxury. At the age of ten, she had run her own wing of the stable. By eighteen, she became the best horsewoman in California's most horsey community. She would rope her own wild horses, break and train them. On a Nevada ranch, where she was visiting, she found a three-day-old leppy, an orphan colt, whose mother had been killed, and brought it up on a bottle. This little devil grew up like a dog and used to break out of its corral and appear at dinner parties or wherever she happened to be.

Ysabel speaks the dog language perfectly, and all animals understand her. She can make anything she sticks in the ground grow and is, generally speaking, a wonder. But she's no mannequin.

I was waiting for her to go out to lunch with me one day, and she was late, which was unusual. I shrieked up the stairs to her. She came down, holding out a bedraggled object.

"What's the matter?" I asked her.

"Ching just had four puppies in my go-away hat on the bottom of the closet."

I didn't ask her why her best hat was on the floor of the closet. Instead, I just stopped at the chicest milliner in Palm Beach and bought her a new one. By the time we got back to the house, the creation looked like her stay-at-home.

This is as accurate a picture as I can draw of the one I really love best in all the world. She has been my pal since that first November morning in 1920 when I met her at the West Palm Beach train station.

In the spring she returned to California, having legally adopted one of Ching's puppies. We never have corresponded. Each fall she would show up without any warning, just as though she had seen me the night before.

Wilson moved from my sheltering roof and built his own house on Worth Avenue, a block from my new apartment. He did the most extraordinary thing, and my admiration is top for his grit. Ten years ago, it was not only a crime to be caught taking dope of any sort, but it was also a crime to try to cure the habit. There was only one thing that one could do legally, and that was give yourself up, be convicted, and sent to prison. There the cure was the most brutal thing and seldom acted as a permanent cure.

Wilson got in touch with a doctor and a nurse in New York whose name I cannot give, or he might be arrested even yet. Arrangements were made for him to be treated. All alone, he left Palm Beach and put himself in the hands of this expert. The course was six days of twilight sleep, and when he came out of that, there were a couple of weeks building up for his nerves.

He came back home looking a little the worse for wear, but he has never touched anything since. For this, my hat is off!

One day I asked him what had made him make up his mind to do it.

"You know that furniture store on Poinsettia Street?" he said. "Well, I wanted a small table, so I stopped in to get one there. The proprietor came out to wait on me. He's a bird who told me he used to be a mortician and embalmer. "You see," he said, "a nice line of caskets went right in fine with the other furniture. I was doing fine. I took a great pride in the work and the like. But then, a cheap lot got into the business and, you know, an artist can't compete with a lot of bums. So, I just dropped the line. I loved to work on a nice old lady who had lived a decent life, but God deliver me from a hophead!"

"What do you mean? Why don't you like to work on them?"

"Well, you know, they won't sit up no matter how much of an artist you are. You can't get no pride out of a job that'll go all to pieces on you."

"What do you care whether you sit up or not when you're dead?" I asked him.

"Well, it kind of got my goat. I made up my mind that I was going to be a sitter. I went over to see the old fellow yesterday to find out how long after you stopped the stuff before you would be all right. It seems they fill you full of something like plaster of Paris. He meant set up like cement."

Irving and Ellin Berlin had taken a house. Anita Loos and her husband, John Emerson, were also in residence. We all saw a lot of one another.

Wilson was nearly fifty, and the girls still thought he was cute, one big brunette especially. I first got on to it when she began patting up Ysabel and suggesting that she ask Wilson to tea. She was a bright, nice girl and only about twenty-three, so I thought I must be wrong. Ysabel and I went into conference and agreed that she had a case. When the big sap began banting, he took off forty pounds and seven years. We knew it was two-sided.

Just at this time a beautiful Viennese blonde showed up. I began to hear that my brother was philandering, which befuddled me a lot. But, in the daytime, he was very dressy and attentive to Mabel. Ysabel, Anita, and I had to keep up on the night and day edition of Wilson's life.

Anita and Ysabel were inseparable. I am sure Wilson had never seen Anita unless she was linked arm-in-arm with Ysabel. Irving and John Emerson, Anita's husband, had both gone to New York on business, when Ellin, Anita, Ray Goetz,[2] and some others, dropped in and dined with us. Each had their bit to dish about the romances.

We had finished dinner and were having coffee in the living room, when Anita said, "It's just the same thing over and over again. I think we ought to throw some life into it. Go to the different extensions of the telephone, and I'll kid him." There were enough of these for each, and Anita rang him up.

In the most sobbing voice I ever heard, she said, "Wilson, is that you, I just had a call from Irving, and he told me that John was on to us."

Anyone but my baby brother would have said, "On to what?" But not so with Wilson. Breathlessly he boomed back, "No! Who told him?"

"I don't know, dear. He's on his way back and gets here on the morning train. I'm leaving for Havana tonight. It's awful. I'm scared to death."

"I'll go with you! What time do you leave? Where are you now? At home! I'll be right over."

"No, wait about twenty minutes until I get rid of the servants."

We all scurried around, piled into cars, and went over to the Emersons', hiding the cars in other people's drives. We hid in the pantry, where we could hear the next act. We had piled up all the empty luggage we could find on the porch. Wilson burst in and clasped Anita to his beltline. Anita is four feet and six inches and Wilson is six feet and four inches.

"My little woman, I bet that dirty little Irving spilled the beans."

There were six heads sticking out of the pantry door, and we almost decapitated poor little Ellin. We all tried to close the door at once, to save her from hearing the tirade that was sure to follow. Although Wilson adored Irving, anyone could suffer when he was dramatizing himself. By this time, it was eleven o'clock, and Anita, making faces at us, began to whimper again.

"Oh, little Willie, I'm so scared. We will have to hurry to catch the three o'clock boat from Miami. You had better go home and pack. I'll pick you up there in an hour."

He departed, and we all began talking at once. By twelve, the rest of the murderers, including Anita who led the parade, marched into Wilson's.

"Hello Willie! We just saw the most wonderful movie, where the villain tried to elope with his best friend's wife."

It was the period just before the boom was called the boom, and we all had money and were happy, full of pranks and joy.

Mrs. Edward McLean of Washington and I had met when she was just a girl in Newport. Then, her name was Walsh. Although I had seen her here in Palm Beach, it had been only fleeting glances. Her husband was very strict and hardly ever let her out of his sight for a minute. He wouldn't let her dine out, or even tea. For fifteen years she had stayed home, where she gave enormous dinners to senators, presidents, and diplomats and grew dreary and political. But there was some rift in the loot. For the first time, I began seeing her at parties, ablaze with jewels and looking like a hailstorm splattered with blood. On top of the Hope Diamond, the Star of the East, bracelets, and necklaces, she would wear the McLean rubies.

Glistening like this one night, she said, "Addison, did you hear Borah's speech[3] last night on the radio?"

"No, I haven't a radio."

"You haven't got a radio? Well, I'll send you one tomorrow."

She went on to tell me about the speech. The party was breaking up, and Ysabel came in to tell me not to forget that I had promised to take her on to the Dirty Nellie to dance.

"Where is that? I wish you would ask me."

"Come along. It's the Daneli Garden. It's not so very smart, but they have the best music, and it is a lot of fun."

We went, stayed until four o'clock, and had a fine time. She had two detectives with her. Even then, I didn't feel too comfortable with all that junk on her. For although this was a delightful place, it was not exactly what you might call exclusive.

I was terribly busy the next day, and at five thirty I flopped into my big chair for a breathing spell. The butler came in, followed by two electricians carrying a radio, and the McLean's butler.

"The madam sent you this radio and asked me to apologize about it not being exactly new. She found that it would take several days before they could get you one, so she sent the one out of her dressing room. Where do you want it put, sir?"

"Right alongside my chair, where I can turn it off. I hate radios."

They fussed for half an hour, throwing wires out of windows, and tinkering with thingamabobs. I thought they would drive me mad while it spluttered, rattled, and hissed at me.

"Joe, I think one of the tubes is blown."

They opened it up, and there lay at least $5 million worth of jewels.

She had been too tired to fuss with a safe and just dumped them into the radio. There they all were. And just my luck, three witnesses, or I might be living in central China now.

10

Ysabel had spent the winter with me, and in the summer of 1923, she talked me into going to California with her.

I hadn't been home for twenty years and felt I was making a sacrifice of my usual European trip. Even so, I threw selfishness to the winds and rediscovered the Pacific slope. I had heard that fine roads had replaced the axle-deep ruts of yore, so I telegraphed ahead for a Cadillac to meet me at the St. Francis Hotel in San Francisco.

It was bright moonlight as we slid down the Sierras. I kept napping and peeking until we reached Sacramento and then fell into a sound sleep.

Early in the morning, Ysabel beat on the door separating out compartments. "We pass through Benicia in half an hour. You better get dressed and have a look at it."

Dear old Benicia: what memories. It was my birthplace. I remember my tearful departure when we broke up home and left for Central America. Great broad streets, beautiful fields, and magnificent buildings. I hurried out onto the platform as we struck the too-meager suburbs, or were they the slums? My heavens, no. It was Benicia itself. The dirtiest stinking little town I had ever seen. I staggered back into the drawing room and drew down the shades.

With all the joy of returning to the home of the Mizners, where their wit and escapades had echoed through the city, I stepped up to the desk at the St. Francis Hotel. With a flourish, I signed my name in a bold, clear hand. The old clerk swung the register around, studied the name for a minute, and said, "What sort of rooms do you wish, *Mr. Mitzner*?"

My God! They had even forgotten the name. I slunk off behind an old bellhop, who flung open the door and said, "I'll see that your trunks are sent up at once, *Mr. Miser*."

The telephone rang. "This is Mr. Cohen speaking. This you, Adolph? I want to speak to Mr. *Missenberg*."

I remembered Wilson's return to Benicia, after he had the triumphs of *Alias Jimmy Valentine* and *The Deep Purple*, two plays that had tremendous success in New York. He jumped off the train at Benicia with clapping of hands and bubbling over with delight. He, too, was home. There was no one at the station but Mike, the old hackman. Wilson slapped him on the back and was about to hug him. The old man had a repellent expression on his lips. "Chickens will come home to roost," he sneered. Wilson was just able to swing onto the last car as the train pulled out, and he has never been back.

William was the only member of the family still alive in California.[1] I called him in Oakland, wondering if he would remember the name. After more than twenty years, he recognized my voice. This made up for the rest, but when he came into the lobby to have lunch with us, Ysabel had to nudge me and say, "Uncle William." When I had seen him last, he was the pride of the family for looks: six feet, three inches, straight, and an athlete. Now, a heavy, old man on crutches hobbled up. Fifteen years before, he had broken his kneecap, and fellow surgeons had completed the disaster for him. His outlook was rural.

My secretary came in to tell me the car would be delivered at two. William wouldn't believe that any Mizner could have a traveling secretary, and I had to spend the rest of the day in terror for fear he would see my valet. It's just as well he didn't see him. Bedford was very severe with me. Looking over my shoulder, when I registered, he said, in a very superior tone, "There is only one 'l' in valet."

In the afternoon, Ysabel and I tried out the new car and were stopped by a traffic light. There was a big monkey in a window. Ysabel said, "That's Robinson's. He has the most wonderful animals in the world."

"Let's go in."

We did, and I came out with a kinkajou, which I needed just as much as I did a sore thumb. It now looked as though I would have to add an animal trainer to the expedition. Ysabel always traveled with Dumpy, who was the outcome of a misalliance of the black chow puppy I had given her and, she thought, a traveling man in the shape of an Australian sheepdog. Anyway, he was sort of a cotton-back chow who would have been degraded by sitting in a cabinet meeting, for he was really intelligent. The kinkajou is a nocturnal thing and curled up and went to sleep all day. Gosh, at night!

We dined with some friends of Ysabel's. Their parents, grandparents, or maybe their great-grandparents, had been pals of mine. Glibly, I began asking about old playmates.

"Where is Pearl ________?"

"Where is she, Harry? In Agnew's or a private asylum?"

"And Dave ________?"

"Oh, he's in San Quentin! Got ten years for forging his sister's name."

"And where is Walter ________?"

"I don't know. He's been dead ten years."

After that we discussed the big trees, which are the oldest living things in the world. They were there when God was a whistling boy and found that two of those were dead.

I was only forty-eight and acting like eighteen. Back at the hotel, I drew aside the old doorman and asked about the ladies of another set, who had lived for pleasure. Even if some of the older ones who had worn the mantle of authority had passed on, surely some of the younger ones I had known would have taken their places. The old man recognized me and squinted at me in a disapproving way.

"Say! Don't you know that about twenty years ago they closed up all those places? It was about the time that all you Mizners left here. I don't mean that your leaving had anything to do with it exactly."

"But what happened to all the girls?"

"Oh, they had to marry, bankers, oil men, and mining men. Lots of them come here, richer than ever."

It was quite late by now. The old man and I sat down on the cold granite steps and revised the Social Register. Six of them had married into the English peerage. One was a French duchess, two were Italian princesses, and 90 percent of them had married well. You see that the straight and narrow path is not the best, especially after you have got your training on the big, wide, winding roads, and have gotten strength enough to stand the climb up the steep goat path.

The next morning, we were to take our first trip in my new car. It was a beauty. A coupe, upholstered in dark blue velour, with a shelf behind the seat for Dumpy and the kinkajou. In great style, we started off. The car ran like melted butter. We got as far as the cemeteries on the San Mateo Road, when people began shouting and pointing. I thought they were admiring our splendor. Ysabel turned to wave to some friends who passed.

"You'd better stop! We look like a comet. The darn thing's afire!"

Before we had come to a standstill, another car had stopped. One man pulled a sprinkler off a grave and was dousing the flames while others threw dirt. They put out the blaze but made a mud pie of the car.

One of the amateur firemen said, "Evidently, you're a stranger out here. You can't use your brakes on these long hills.

Go into second and only use the brake a little now and then." Being a stranger in my own land, I took his advice.

We were lunching with the Bill Crockers,[2] back of Burlingame, and were in a hurry so couldn't have the car washed. After lunch, Ruth Crocker said, "Where is Dumpy? It's the first time I've seen you without him."

"I let him out for a run."

A look of horror came over Ruth's face.

"You had better get him at once. We have had a rat catcher here all morning, and he has covered the place with Rose's Rat Poison!"

Everyone ran for the door. Instantly, on Ysabel's call. Dumpy came prancing up, and we all went back to our coffee, with sighs of relief.

On our way back to the city, we passed Burlingame and were out on a road between that beautiful park and the outer edges of South San Francisco when the worst happened.

"Stop! Dumpy is sick!"

As though I didn't know it on every inch of me.

"Stop nothing! Where is the nearest drugstore or grocer?"

The brakes held as we almost crashed the doors of a soda pop stand.

"Give me a couple dozen eggs and a pan."

The woman thought we were crazy and got a move on her. I set Ysabel to cracking the eggs and saving the whites, while I got Dumpy out of the car and laid him on the ground. We poured the gooey mess down him and then squeezed him. The poison had cooked the eggs like a quick fire. Several times we repeated the operation and wound up by filling him full of milk. The poor fellow began wagging his tail limply, and the glassy look seemed to fade out of his eyes as he sat up.

If the outside of the car looked awful, you should have seen the inside. But I never liked Pullman plush anyway. You can't slide on it without having your pants bifurcate you to the armpits. So, I had slipcovers made. Now that the newness had worn off, we were much more at home in the car and planned longer trips.

On our way to Monterey, we stopped to have lunch with some friends of Ysabel's.

"They are the ones who have been so nice about storing my furniture," she said. "We have an hour before lunch. Let's stop at the barn on our way up the drive. I want to see how it's getting on."

Stacked high to the rafters was a heterogeneous mess. I had on white flannels, and it was not hard to see that I was wading in fleas. But she thought everything looked all right, and I didn't try to disabuse her.

After lunch, we sailed along over perfect roads and struck Monterey at about six o'clock.

"Where do we stay?"

"The Lodge at Pebble Beach. It is the old Seventeen-Mile-Drive, you remember it! Sam Morse[3] has turned it into a residence park, like Tuxedo. The lodge is just like a home. Everybody is so nice to me, and a lot of friends are staying there."

The kinkajou was named Neuter because no one could be sure what else to call it. At the San Mateo Polo Club, where we had stayed, Neuter had jumped out of the window one night and disappeared. I didn't notice that it wasn't in the basket when I went to bed. About one o'clock there was a timid knock at my door.

"This is Coleman. You know, I'm the steward. Have you lost anything, Mr. Mizner, 'cause there is some kind of wild animal trying to break in my window, and my wife is scared to death?"

I opened the door, and there stood Coleman with a polo mallet.

"If it ain't yours, will you help me kill it?"

I looked in the basket. Poor little Neuter had gone, evidently, for a stroll and was now trying to get back in again. When we got to Coleman's quarters, Mrs. Coleman was making jabs at Neuter with a broom, and he was becoming enraged. I opened the screen and took Neuter in my arms. We all settled down again for the night.

The first night at the Lodge, I put Neuter in the bathroom when we went down to dine with Jane and Harry Hunt.[4] I heard shrieks and screams at the office and rushed out to find a terrible commotion. The maid had gone into the bathroom with a broom, and Neuter bit her on the leg. After that, it always hated brooms.

Harry and Jane were in the throes of building a house and had been in labor for over a year. From the looks of poor Clarence Tantau, the architect, it appeared like a cesarean to me. They all invited me to a conference after dinner. We fumbled over plans for hours. Had it been as terrible as the Tibetan villa, I would have said it was lovely. For a fact, the plans were really fine.[5]

About midnight Ysabel and I sat down in our little sitting room to watch Neuter eat its banana and to talk.

"What do you think of the plans?"

"They are very good, indeed. The only trouble is the Hunts don't know how to read them."

"I understand that they look like Aztec to me. I would be willing to live in a tepee here. Wouldn't you?"

"Would you rather live here than Burlingame?" I asked.

"Oh, yes. I would rather live here than any place in the world."

The next morning, I was downstairs at six thirty. I found a raised map of Pebble Beach in the lobby and was studying it to see what road I would take for a drive. Marion Hollins came down with her golf bag.[6]

"You practicing to win the championship again?" I asked.

"More or less. It is part of my job now that I am selling real estate here. With the best course west of Chicago, we are trying to attract the golfers and sell them acreage."

"Come along. I'm a sucker. I want to see properties."

She insisted upon getting into her car, as she knew the roads. What a Ben Hur she was. Around corners on one wheel, pointing out the views, across fields for a short cut, and all the time talking lots and sites. Stopping with a jerk here and sliding into a standstill there, with a map in one hand and a price list in the other.

"This is a beautiful piece. It overlooks the ocean, four acres, only $55,000."

On through the great dense pine forest, mounting higher, looking down hundreds of feet to the ocean one minute, and over Carmel Bay to the mountains, which rise thousands of feet into the clear blue sky. Ysabel was right. It is the most beautiful place in the world.

"Let's look at something lower down."

"All the ocean front has been sold down there on the cliffs, where the Monterey cypress are."

"I mean one halfway down."

We whirled down and down.

"Stop."

"What's the matter?" said Marion, as we ground to a standstill.

"How much is this piece?"

"Oh, that's cheap. Only ten thousand an acre, but it's too steep. There isn't any room to build a house on it."

Before lunch I had finished my plans on some wrapping paper, with a foot rule as my only equipment. I had the deed to the property made out in Ysabel's name and made a date with the contractor for two thirty.

I met Tantau in the passage, looking terribly disheartened.

"Cheer up, old man. You'll have your contract signed by tonight."

"Good! When did you see them?" he said, his face writhing in joy.

"I haven't seen them since we left them last night."

The joy died on his lips. I pointed to the bundle of wrapping paper under my arm. "I've got the plans for Ysabel's house here. We are starting to build in the morning. They will get all enthused and won't want her to beat them to it." He still looked downcast, as he moved away.

That afternoon we staked out the house. The next morning, men were at work clearing and making foundation forms. By noon, we were pouring concrete.

The next day Harry signed up.

We went for a week's motor trip and then came back to get a squint at the house. Things were going fine. I passed on trim and plumbing fixtures, and left with, "I'll see you next year."

Ysabel Chase Hollins residence, facade. Padre Lane, Pebble Beach, California. Addison Mizner, architect, 1924.

When I returned, eight months later, Mr. Ruhl met me at the house. Everything was perfect until we went into one of the bathrooms. The only seat in the place was glistening, sparkling, imitation mother-of-pearl.

"That isn't what I ordered!"

"I know, but these are better. They are 10 percent warmer than plain white."

Mr. Ruhl had told Harry Hunt that I was the funniest architect he had ever seen.

"You know, he just walked out on me, after sticking a roll of wrapping paper and a list of timber, plumbing, and things in my hand. He expects me to put it together. All he said was, 'You'd better make a good job of it, or I'll wear it out on you.'"

If I was a bum architect, he was a good contractor, for it all fitted together.

11

It is not my purpose to dish the dirt about people. But some day, if I back into my wrapper and a rocking chair and let myself go, I won't know where to stop.

My huge living room became a sort of salon where everybody who came to Palm Beach came at least once a season. New Year's Day at home had always been eggnog day. Starting with bare boards and wet plaster, I had about ten guests the year we built the club. Now, it had grown to three or four hundred, as people began to realize that December and January were just as fine as February and March. The season had stretched out each year. Instead of the old hotel days, when people came the last of January and left after Washington's Birthday, they were now coming in droves by the first of December.

Although I love my friends and people in general, I have never been a gusher. I am too socially lazy and too busy to bother. In fact, I wouldn't cross the Delaware to meet the signers of the Declaration of Independence. I had become one of the sights, and people flocked in. When they got there, I loved them.

There was one old lady who had told Joan Singer and a few others of my best friends to tell me not to try to be the social leader of Palm Beach on a dollar ninety-eight. She had humped up her rump especially over some royalties who were spending one winter. Being perfectly real people, they loved coming in every afternoon and getting a laugh. For, above all, the wits gathered about Wilson and other amusing hounds that were always there. The result was that the old lady stopped speaking to me.

All the eggnog guests were asked by telephone. Bedford, thinking the quarrel had gone far enough, invited the old lady. I was standing in the living room on New Year's Day when Bedford slipped up to me, whispered that the old lady had arrived and was in the dining room.

"Well, you had better go back and watch the silver."

I didn't know that he had invited her.

Later in the season each year, I gave a musicale to get even with everyone who had asked me out. One of the most important ones was when Madame Frances Alda sang for me.[1] There were about two hundred invited, and three hundred had come. Wilson was slightly in his cups and wasn't dressed, so he stood just outside one of the glass doors on the terrace. He could see and hear Alda without being seen by the audience. As she finished the first half of her program, she made her exit by this door. Wilson greeted her with, "That was wonderful Alda. You've given me a new sensation tonight."

"I wish to God someone would give me one."

"Come along with me, and I'll make you feel as though you had a million canaries picking seed off your stomach."

I've always wondered if you could rent canaries.

One year, I had the New York String Quartet every afternoon for two weeks, from six to seven o'clock. They sat in the middle of the Gothic room, with the lights on their music stands as the only illumination. They played divinely, as daylight died through the soft tints of the colored glass. People came in quietly, without greetings, and sank into big chairs. One felt medieval as the footman stole about lighting great cathedral candles here and there.[2]

Irving Berlin wrote two or three hits on my piano. Jerome Kern, Gershwin, and others would play by the hour in the afternoons. Even Mary Garden sang for me alone.[3] There was always something doing.

On Christmas Eve, Charlie Amory, who had gotten together a choir, serenaded me. It was lovely, looking down into the court where the fountain dripped, and coconut trees spread their huge fronds out on the starry night. All those young faces lit by the flicker of long red tapers took me back to Benicia, where William, trying to kick the boy in front of him, got old Sammy Gray, the Sunday school teacher, by mistake. It turned "We Three Kings of Orient Are" into a battle.

One year I was having a big star sing for me. A few days before the concert she came down with a cold. I telephoned an agent to see if I could get a substitute.

"You are very fortunate Mr. Mizner, for the great Argentine tenor, Senor Mateo del Campo, is passing through. They say he is wonderful."

We came to terms, and I breathed a sigh of relief.

The room was filling up. There was Madame Homer, and over there Alda, and here, Jerry Kern, the Seligmans in the corner.[4] The place was stuffed with music lovers. I introduced my star and told the hushed audience he would open the program with some old Argentine folk songs. Then, fortunately, I retired to the door where I could greet the late guests.

The accompanist rattled off a prelude and then the tenor lit a yap out of him that no amount of bicarbonate of soda could sweeten. It was probably the most horrible sound I had ever heard. I took no chances and broke into a run as I fled. I knocked down people who were just coming in and ran until I was out of breath. Then I realized how cowardly I was. I sneaked back and grabbed my squawker.

"The place is on fire," I whispered to him in Spanish. "I would like to get the people out as quickly and quietly as possible." I didn't have to yell fire to my guests, for they were already jamming the exits, as though someone had thrown in a stink bomb.

Addison Mizner apartment, living room. Via Mizner.

Moral—always hear your tenors first.

The charm of dropping in for the afternoons was that you never knew who was going to be there. It might be Fannie Ward in the spring of her sixtieth year looking eighteen, or the curator of a museum, but it was generally amusing.[5] The inner circle was the one, of course, I enjoyed best. We had many laughs together.

But it wasn't all entertainment. I was always up and doing before six in the morning. I could get some work done before office hours. I had a stream of people to see all morning, bossing jobs all afternoon, and by five thirty I was tired. At a quarter of eight, when Bedford came in to tell me I was dining out and where, I was always rebellious and dragged myself into the elevator, about to die. When I would get to a party, I always enjoyed it.

AFTERWORD

Despite his failing health during those final months, Addison Mizner recalled the music from those carefree days he spent at Palm Beach. Mizner's memoir ended as he stood at the brink of his career's next phase that he believed would secure his fortune and legacy but instead had sparked the economic collapse of his wide-ranging ventures.

Just months after the 1924 season, his Mizner Development Company unveiled its plan for Boca Raton, promising "an entire city which would capture the picturesque appeal of Old Spain with the world's most complete and artistic hotel." Fueled by

Boca Raton, 1925. Wilson Mizner, Marie Dressler, and Addison Mizner.

more than $5 million of capital stock and regarded as the driving force of Palm Beach County's development, Mizner's syndicate failed eleven months later.

"My dear Addison," wrote Paris Singer, in a letter to Mizner dated April 19, 1926,[1] "Wilson has just told me that you wanted me to let you have some money. I am sorry that I have to refuse, as money is scarce these days." Two months after contractors began filing liens in Boca Raton, Mizner was forced to give up his interest in the development company. Buried beneath a pyramid of creditor demands and civil lawsuits, he reorganized, separating Mizner Industries from his architectural practice and other interests. He began leasing his treasured Via Mizner apartment during the winter season as he sought to keep his various manufacturing workshops engaged.

As an influx of architects generated a more competitive setting, Mizner expanded production at his Bunker Road workshops. Believing coquina would replace molded cement blocks as construction materials, he established a quarry keystone facility in the Florida Keys and processing plants on Florida's east and west coasts. Large blocks of stone were transported to his workshops where a fifty-horsepower saw cut the rock into building and paving stones. Again, Mizner's entrepreneurism was threatened by market conditions, as the Wall Street crash curbed construction.

Although Mizner's Palm Beach mansions had conferred on him an iconic eminence, the vacillating economy was shifting taste away from Mizner's large-scale works in favor of less elaborate architectural styles. Never restrained by a prescribed architectural theory, like Beaux-Arts-trained architects' use of rigid conventions for floor plans and facades, Mizner's resort style grew out of his client's needs and pleasures as well as the project's unique location.

Mizner Industries, Bunker Road. Quarry keystone manufacturing plant.

His loss of professional footing was made worse by health issues, legal tangles, and diminished resources. Nonetheless, Mizner's wavering financial status never affected his social popularity. He continued to engage in civic and social affairs as well as host private dinners and his annual New Year's Day open house. He rejoined the influential art jury that approved building plans for the town.

Determined to secure Addison's historical legacy, Alice DeLamar funded and produced a monograph of Mizner's Palm Beach houses and buildings in 1927. DeLamar not only conceived the book and parleyed a national publisher, but she also selected the photos and wrote the captions. Along with an essay on Mizner's talents by Paris Singer and an introduction by Ida Tarbell, DeLamar engaged noted lensman F. E. Geisler for the photography.

Via Parigi. Worth Avenue, 1925. Shops with apartments and office tower, under construction.

In addition to a standard bookshelf volume, an oversized limited-edition publication bound in red Moroccan leather was published for patrons whose support would aid in underwriting the most comprehensive visual record of Mizner's Palm Beach work. The book was published before Mizner's houses were altered, damaged during the 1928 hurricane, or demolished. *Architectural Forum* magazine reviewed the book, calling it "one of the most handsomely designed and printed contributions to an architect's library to appear in many a day."

During the summer of 1928, Addison Mizner wrote a letter to Alice DeLamar from his Carmel Valley cottage: "My dearest Alice, I have been so ill since the book took shape that I have never made it quite clear how much I appreciated the greatest compliment ever paid a living architect."[2]

Singer Building, 1925. Royal Palm Way at The Society of The Four Arts Plaza.

That same year, Mizner's office designed several notable residences outside of Palm Beach. In Montecito, he created Casa Bienvenita, a forty-room, seventeen thousand square-foot villa for a former New York client. Near Philadelphia, he conceived a stylistic derivative of Playa Riente called La Ronda, a large-scale Gothic-inspired showplace. As developer Clarence Geist was redeveloping Mizner's foreclosed Cloister Inn into the Boca Raton Club, Geist's lawyer, Jerome Gedney, retained Mizner to design L'Encantada in Manalapan. Among other commissions during this period, Mizner drew plans for The Cloister resort at Sea Island, Georgia, named for his failed Boca Raton hotel.

The September 1928 hurricane wreaked havoc on Palm Beach, causing several Mizner mansions to undergo structural redesign by other architects. The following year, Mizner suffered an immeasurable loss. His nephew and manager of Mizner Industries, Horace Chase Jr., died in an airplane crash. Joseph Widener and Mike Vanderbilt passed over Mizner's plans, selecting Treanor & Fatio to design their newest mansions.

As demand for Mizner's work declined, the town of Palm Beach selected Mizner's design for its memorial plaza and fountain. An aesthetic focal point adjacent to the town's civic buildings, Mizner's plan was inspired as much by Alhambra models as he was influenced by Ohan Berberyan's Jardin Latin fountain on Peruvian Avenue. In addition, Mizner's office, supervised by architect Byron Simonson, drew up the plans for E. R. Bradley's lakefront Embassy Club on Royal Palm Way. The Palm Beach Company retained Mizner for additional Phipps Plaza shops along South County Road, including the E. F. Hutton Building. Mizner's longtime patron, Edith Oliver Rea, commissioned him to rebuild her gardens and design a loggia addition at Lagomar.

During the first week of January 1930, Addison Mizner and Paris Singer lunched together at the Everglades Club, the once close friends meeting after a lengthy estrangement. Soon after, Singer and his wife, Joan, departed Palm Beach for a houseboat on the Nile and their Cap Ferrat villa in the south of France. As his final mansion, Casa Coe da Sol, was built in St. Petersburg, Florida, Mizner filed for personal involuntary bankruptcy in 1931. With the Everglades Club's future still uncertain, headlines reported Paris Singer's death in London in late June 1932.

Soon after, Mizner left Palm Beach and returned to his home in Carmel, California. He had expressed the notion of moving permanently to Carmel to be near his niece and family for several years. In mid-October at Pebble Beach, Mizner's niece Ysabel and husband, McKim Hollins, christened their son, Kim Mizner Hollins, with two godfathers: one, their son's namesake,

Addison Mizner; the other, family friend Harry Hunt. While Mizner was still in California, the Sears Publishing Company released his autobiographical book, *The Many Mizners*.

Shortly before Christmas Day, he returned to his Via Mizner apartment. His niece Ysabel arrived in January to supervise his care. At the end, with his fortune gone and living on borrowed money, his death on February 5, 1933, made national headlines. The day after, the Town Council of Palm Beach renamed Town Hall Plaza as Mizner Plaza, paying tribute "in memorial to the artistic debt that Palm Beach owes to the late Addison Mizner."

Addison Mizner's memoir captures the spirit and tenor of Palm Beach during the time when the resort attracted many of the twentieth century's most influential and legendary personalities. With his remaining houses and buildings recognized as landmarks, Mizner's name appears on street signs, schools, and shopping centers, in gratitude for having created and inspired what is acknowledged as the Palm Beach style.

—Augustus Mayhew III

ARCHITECTURAL TIMELINE

EDITOR'S NOTE:

The Architectural Timeline lists Addison Mizner's Palm Beach commissions chronologically arranged from 1918 until 1924. Each year's register is followed by photographs from the Historical Society's collection that showcase Mizner's architectural design and, in some cases, include furniture and artifacts from Mizner Industries.

REFERENCES:

Curl, Donald W. *Mizner's Florida: American Resort Architecture.* Cambridge: The MIT Press, 1984.

Historical Society of Palm Beach County. *Directory of Architectural Drawings & Materials.* West Palm Beach: Historical Society of Palm Beach County, 1999.

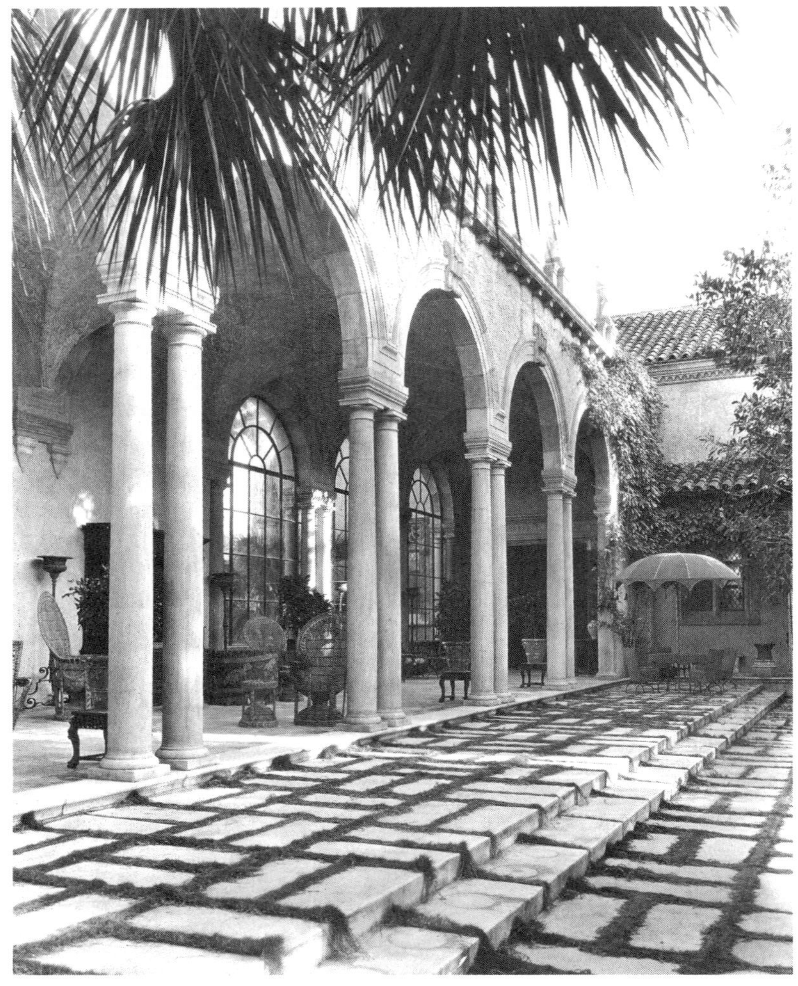

910 South Ocean Boulevard, loggia. 1923. Casa Florencia, Preston and Florence Satterwhite residence.

Palm Beach: 1918–1924

1918

356 Worth Avenue, Everglades Club. Clubhouse, villas, and garage.

Everglades Club, 1918. View from Worth Avenue looking southeast. Original clubhouse waterfront elevation on Singer Basin.

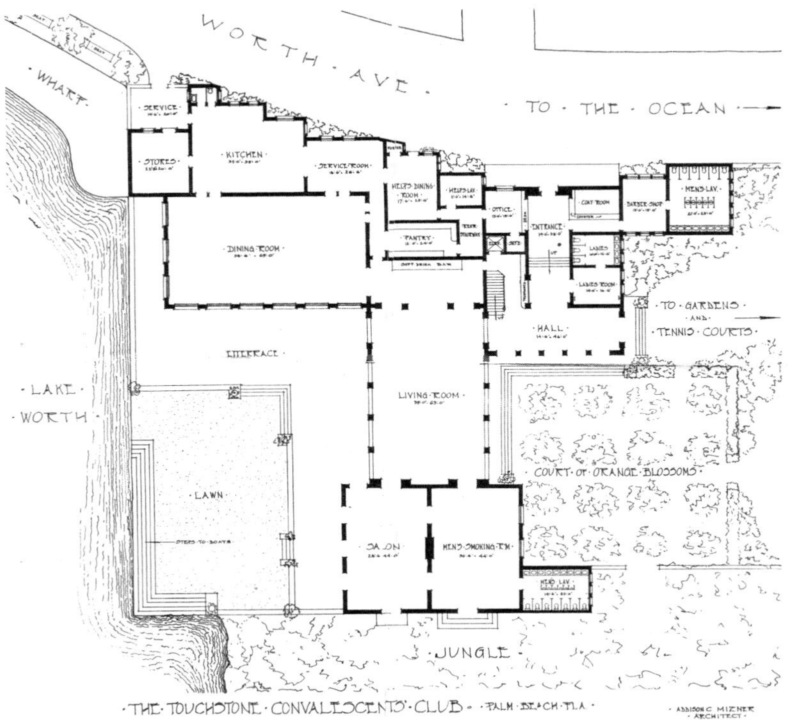

Touchstone Convalescents' Club, line drawing. Clubhouse plan, 1918. Addison Mizner, architect.

1919

356 Worth Avenue, Everglades Club.

348 North County Road, El Mirasol. Residence for Edward T. Stotesbury. Demolished.

455 North County Road, Amado. Residence for Charles Munn.

473 North County Road, Louwana. Residence for Gurnee Munn.

189 Sunset Avenue, Villa Yalta. Residence/Teahouse for E. Clarence Jones. Demolished.

720 South Ocean Boulevard, El Solano. Residence for Addison Mizner sold to Harold S. Vanderbilt.

Everglades Club. Original Worth Avenue entrance.

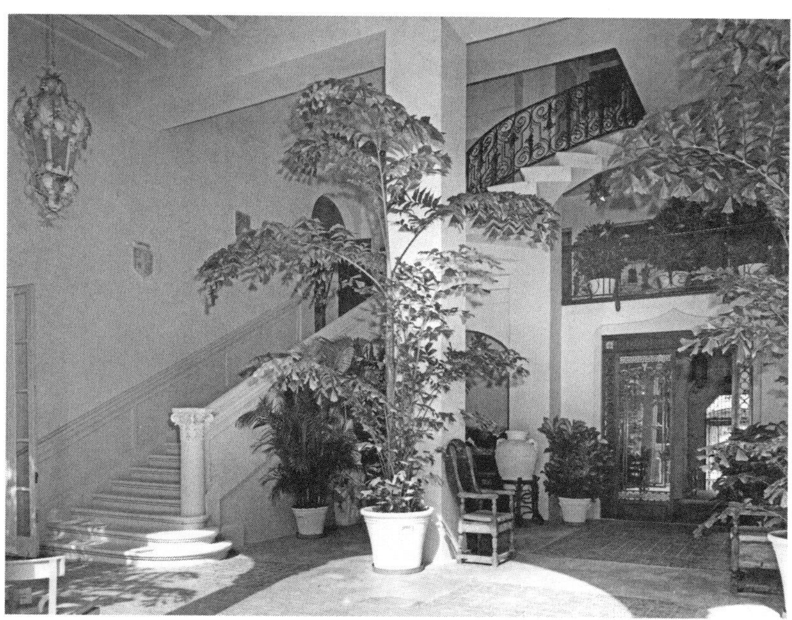

Everglades Club, interior central staircase.

Everglades Club, dining room.

*El Mirasol,
patio balcony.*

El Mirasol, loggia.

El Mirasol, breakfast loggia.

El Mirasol, dining porch.

Amado, east elevation.

Amado, entrance hall.

Aerial. Left, Amado, built for Charles and Mary Munn; right, Louwana, built for Gurnee and Marie Louise Wanamaker Munn.

1920

111 Dunbar Road, Costa Bella. Residence for Elizabeth H. G. Slater.

1200 South Ocean Boulevard, La Billucia. Residence for Willey and Lucy Kingsley.

La Billucia, interior.

1921

450 Worth Avenue, Casa dei Leoni. Residence for Leonard Thomas.

121 El Bravo Way. Residence for Hon. Charles J. Winn.

582 South Ocean Boulevard, Audita. Residence for Alfred and Elizabeth Kay.

102 Jungle Road, Concha Marina. Residence for Addison Mizner sold to George Sloane.

434 North County Road, Casa Bendita, Residence for John S. Phipps. Demolished.

163 Seminole Avenue, Villa dei Fiori. Residence for O. Frank Woodward.

Casa dei Leoni, south elevation.

Casa dei Leoni, entrance. Worth Avenue elevation.

Casa dei Leoni, living room.

Above: Concha Marina, courtyard.

Casa Bendita, covered pool. John and Margarita Grace Phipps residence.

Casa Bendita, living room.

Casa Bendita, living room.

Villa dei Fiori. Original facade, west elevation facing North County Road.

1922

135 Grace Trail. Residence for Joseph M. Cudahy.

1426 South Ocean Boulevard. Lakefront residence for Alice DeLamar. Design plans rendered in Mizner office. Demolished.

150 South Ocean Boulevard. Residence for Madame Jeanette Gais. Demolished.

1800 South Ocean Boulevard, Sin Cuidado. Addison Mizner residence sold to Edward S. Moore. Demolished.

112 Seminole Avenue. Residence for William Gray Warden.

480 Worth Avenue, Villa des Cygnes. Residence for Barclay Warburton.

182 South Ocean Boulevard, Residence for Walter G. Mitchell. Demolished.

Sin Cuidado, living room.

Sin Cuidado, living room.

Sin Cuidado, portrait room.

Sin Cuidado, portrait room with fireplace.

Warden House. Built for Standard Oil scion William Gray Warden, the house has since been converted into condominium units.

Villa des Cygnes, lakefront south elevation.

Villa des Cygnes, Original Worth Avenue elevation.

1923

150 South Ocean Boulevard, Villa del Sarmiento. Residence for A. J. Drexel Biddle Jr.

280 North Ocean Boulevard. Residence for Daniel H. Carstairs.

800 South County Road, Casa de los Ensueños. Residence for Arthur B. Claflin.

947 North Ocean Boulevard, Playa Riente. Residence for Joshua Cosden. Demolished.

160 Barton Avenue. Residence for Angier Biddle Duke.

2401 North Ocean Boulevard, Gulf Stream. Gulf Stream Golf Club.

Royal Palm Way and South Ocean Boulevard, La Fontana. Residence for George Luke Mesker. Demolished.

337 Worth Avenue, office and studio for Addison Mizner.

401 North Ocean Boulevard, Heamaw. Additions for Henry C. Phipps. Demolished.

100 El Brillo Way, Villa Tranquillo. Residence for De Grimm Renfro.

138 North Ocean Boulevard, Sunrise Villa. Additions for J. Leonard Replogle. Demolished.

910 South Ocean Boulevard, Casa Florencia. Residence for Dr. Preston Pope Satterwhite. Demolished.

110 Dunbar Avenue, Villa Flora. Residence for Edward Shearson.

942 South Ocean Boulevard, Casa Joseto. Residence for Joseph Speidel. Demolished.

1113 North Ocean Boulevard, La Querida. Residence for L. Rodman Wanamaker II.

548 North County Road, The Towers. Residence for William M. Wood. Demolished.

North Lake Trail at Seminole Avenue. Henri Bendel store. Demolished.

Villa del Sarmiento, under construction. East elevation, original entrance.

Villa del Sarmiento, aerial.

Carstairs house, entrance.

Carstairs house, courtyard and fountain.

Carstairs house, living room with patterned tile floor.

Carstairs house, central staircase and hall.

Casa de los Ensueños, Venetian bridge.

Playa Riente, entrance gate on North Ocean Boulevard.

Playa Riente, living room.

Playa Riente, dining room. Murals, Achille Angeli, artist.

Playa Riente, ballroom. Murals, Jose Maria Sert, artist.

Duke-Bache House, ballroom. Commissioned for Angier Buchanan Duke, the house at 160 Barton Avenue was not completed until after Duke's death, when it was bought by Jules Bache.

La Fontana, east elevation overlooking South Ocean Boulevard.

La Fontana, courtyard staircase.

Casa Florencia's front entrance.

Above: Casa Florencia.

Casa Florencia, staircase.

Casa Florencia, dining room.

Casa Florencia, living room.

Villa Flora, 260 North Ocean Boulevard. Entrance faces north on Dunbar Road.

Villa Flora, courtyard and fountain.

Villa Flora, dining room.

Villa Flora, living room.

La Querida, the residence of L. Rodman Wanamaker II. Photograph by Tracy Trumbull.

The Towers, aerial view with east elevation.

1924

337–341 Worth Avenue Worth Avenue, arcade for shops. Mizner five-story tower with apartments, studio, and Via Mizner shops with second-story apartments.

1560 South Ocean Boulevard, Lagomar. Residence for John Magee.

1820 South Ocean Boulevard, Collado Hueco. Residence for Paul Moore.

237 Worth Avenue. Residence for Wilson Mizner.

238–240–246 South County Road. The Plaza shops and apartments for the Palm Beach Company.

288 South County Road. Palm Way Building. Shops and apartments for Ocean and Lake Realty Company.

South Lake Trail, between Seaview and Royal Palm Way. Club Montmartre.

Left, Mizner shopping arcade, plaza, and architectural studio. Right, Five-story tower. 337–341 Worth Avenue.
AUGUSTUS MAYHEW III

Addison Mizner apartment, dining room. Via Mizner.

Worth Avenue second-floor terrace with arcade between Addison Mizner's five-story building and two-story shops and architectural studio, 337–341 Worth Avenue.

Lagomar, east elevation.

Lagomar, aerial view.

Lagomar, arched side entrance elevation with elaborate staircase entrance.

Lagomar, interior.

Collado Hueco, south elevation.

The Plaza shops and apartments, Palm Beach Company owner, South County Road.

Phipps Plaza, courtyard arcade with balconies.

Phipps Plaza, interior courtyard.

Club Montmartre, architectural rendering. Demolished after a fire destroyed the club.

MIZNER INDUSTRIES

The necessity for Addison Mizner and Paris Singer to produce their own construction materials to build the Everglades Club due to wartime limitations became the impetus after the war for launching Mizner Industries. With the Everglades Club's design heralded as Palm Beach's architectural prototype, Mizner Industries quickly grew into the area's major resource for essential and ornamental building materials that nearly every South Florida architect and builder used. At the peak of the 1920s boom, Addison Mizner's various business interests employed seven hundred personnel and twenty-five architectural draftsmen with offices in Florida and New York.

This spiraling development began during the summer and fall of 1918, when Paris Singer used the Novelty Works, a West Palm Beach subsidiary of the Dade Lumber Company, to supply building materials for the construction of the large-scale convalescents' facility for shell-shocked soldiers. Because of the volume of materials needed for the clubhouse and villas, Singer leased the entire Novelty Works complex in West Palm Beach until December 1918.

Upon completion of the club, and having made plans for further building, Singer organized the Los Manos Pottery & Tuileries on South Dixie Highway in West Palm Beach. The facility was named for the site of the Parisian tile factories where the Jardin des Tuileries was built. During the summer of 1919, as Mizner's architectural practice developed, he hired his nephew Horace Chase Jr. to manage the workshop complex located on West Palm Beach's Bunker Road. The following winter, Singer sold Los Manos to Mizner, who renamed it Las Manos Potteries. Mizner began with three kilns, one mule, and a few workmen, establishing Las Manos as the first division of what became Mizner Industries. In addition, Mizner incorporated a parent company, Addison Mizner, Inc., for his professional practice and an import and manufacturing concern that he named Antigua Shops, Inc.

As demand for Mizner's work flourished, he built additional kilns and imported distinctive Georgia clay. Along with roof tiles, he added the production of floor tiles and varieties of pottery. As early as July 1920, architect Martin L. Hampton specified "Las Manos old-style, handmade, roof tiles" for a Palm Island mansion on Miami Beach.[1] In 1923, glazing kilns and cast stone workshops were added.

For his floor tiles, Mizner devised a spectrum of colors from a light pink to a burnt brown through a process of trial and error while mixing, drying, and firing the tiles. At first, he was able to produce thirteen thousand tiles every four days. With additional kilns and craftsmen, he offered floor tiles in thirteen colors: Mizner blue, light blue, Valencia blue, light green, green, neutral green, Mizner yellow, orange, red, brown, blue, blue-black, and black. Along with his Bunker Road workshops in West Palm Beach and Worth Avenue offices, Mizner added a pottery shop at Phipps Plaza on South County Road.[2]

Additional workshop areas at the Bunker Road facility were reserved for blacksmiths, who forged wrought-iron gates, lanterns, and andirons patterned after Spanish and Italian models; and skilled woodworkers, who modeled furniture on medieval and Renaissance imports. By 1923, Mizner's manufactured historically correct furnishings were known to have a properly aged look. Skilled masonry workers transformed concrete-molded architectural forms into a semblance of sixteenth-century carved-stone details.

During the late 1920s, despite Mizner's financial volatility, he diversified and expanded his manufacturing concerns. He set up a quarry keystone plant with limestone trucked from leased quarries on Windley Key near Islamorada and in Ellenton on Florida's west coast. Following the death of his nephew Horace Chase, who had managed the Bunker Road facility, Hugo G. Wagner became Mizner's superintendent in 1928.

Wagner, along with investor John Shephard, had bought Mizner's Woodite production company. Woodite was a synthetic building material made of wood shavings, fibers, and plaster that could be nailed, painted, and sawed to look like authentic, aged wood. When Wagner left Mizner Industries in June 1930 to establish Wagner Stone Works, E. C. Peters, who had worked for Mizner, took over Mizner Industries.

Upon Mizner's death in February 1933, and with his personal estate having filed bankruptcy proceedings two years earlier, Mizner Industries was already in receivership, and involuntary bankruptcy proceedings had already begun. During that spring, Mizner Industries' assets were sold at a sheriff's bankruptcy sale to E. C. Peters, who renamed the company Mizner Products Inc. Several years later, Mizner Products was retitled E. C. Peters Inc. When the need for decorative cast stone waned during wartime, Peters manufactured manhole covers and torpedoes.

He sold his company in 1964 to the Natural Slate & Cast Stone Company, established by E. B. Walton. Along with the 533 Bunker Road site, Walton opened a showroom on Royal Palm Way. The Walton-owned company's manager, James Mannion, later acquired the facility, operating it as Mannion Cast Stone until the late 1970s. At that time, he liquidated the existing original Mizner molds and moved the company from its original Bunker Road site.

While Mizner's estate attorney, E. Harris Drew, and his longtime office manager and his estate's coexecutor, Madena Galloway, were able to convey Mizner's architectural practice to longtime architect William Manly King, the disposition of Via Mizner's multistory shops, offices, and apartment tower became a long, drawn-out undertaking. During the summer of 1936, Via Mizner's apartments and shops were deeded to another entity named Addison Mizner, Inc., organized by a West Palm Beach real estate firm that immediately remortgaged the property. Three years later, that entity was foreclosed.

As further reorganization proceedings were taking place, court documents published in 1940 announced a public sale of not only the real estate but also all the furnishings and attachments found in Mizner's apartment and offices. Court-ordered appraisals indicated Mizner's furnishings were predominantly authentic Spanish and Italian Renaissance antiques, not the factory-made replicas fabricated at the Bunker Road workshops.

After the properties were cleared, Mizner's tower and Via Mizner were sold for $77,000 to Arthur O. "Archie" Edwards in April 1944. The developer of the town of Palm Beach Shores on Singer Island and the Stotesbury Park subdivision, Edwards was a highly regarded London hotelier and a member of the Everglades Club's proxy committee. The following year, rather than retain the property, Edwards sold the Via Mizner holdings for $122,500 to Rosemor, Inc., a New York company organized by Rose and Mortimer Sachs.

Despite Addison Mizner's financial misfortune, today's collectors value the bygone furnishings and unique artifacts produced during the 1920s by Mizner Industries with the same appreciation for craftsmanship as found in centuries-old museum pieces. Addison Mizner's architectural legacy and manufacturing enterprises remain among the area's most valuable trademarks, iconic endeavors that have made Palm Beach County an ultimate destination.

Mizner Industries, Bunker Road outdoor showroom. Paris Singer and Addison Mizner began Las Manos Pottery with a few kilns producing roof and floor tiles that Mizner's vision and skills expanded into Mizner Industries, Palm Beach County's largest business during the 1920s.

Wood carver. Mizner Industries, Bunker Road workshop.

Cast stone artisans. Mizner Industries, Bunker Road workshop.

Furniture craftsmen. Mizner Industries, Bunker Road workshop.

Wrought-iron fabricators. Mizner Industries, Bunker Road workshop.

Las Manos Pottery and Mizner Industries cast stone architectural products were sold in a Via Mizner shop.

On Thursday afternoon, February 9, 1933, at 4 p.m., several hundred of Addison Mizner's friends, clients, and craftsmen crowded into his apartment for a memorial service following his death the week before. "He hated sham, he hated hypocrisy, he hated the unreal, the untrue," eulogized Bishop Nathaniel Seymour Thomas, amid bouquets of golden roses that filled the rooms where he lived and where he died.

Addison Mizner apartment tower with ground-floor arcade and second-floor terrace. Via Mizner at Worth Avenue.
Augustus Mayhew III

BIBLIOGRAPHY

Newspapers

California Digital Newspaper Collection (University of California, Riverside, Center for Bibliographic Studies and Research)

New York Sun

New York Times

Palm Beach Daily News

Palm Beach Post, 1916–1933

Plain Talk, 1911–1914

Books

Curl, Donald W. *Mizner's Florida: American Resort Architecture*. Cambridge, MA: MIT Press, 1984.

Florida Architecture of Addison Mizner. Foreword by Paris Singer. "Appreciation of a Layman" by Ida Tarbell. New York: William Helburn, 1928.

Mizner, Addison. *The Many Mizners*. New York: Sears, 1932.

Periodicals

Boyd, John Taylor Jr. "The Florida House: Addison Mizner, Architect, Recounts the Birth of the New Florida Architecture at Palm Beach." *Arts & Decoration 32* (January 1930): 37–40.

"First Shell-Shock Club in America at Palm Beach." *Arts & Decoration* (October 1918): 7.

"Gulf Stream Golf Club, Palm Beach, Florida." *Architectural Forum 42* (March 1925): 25–27.

"House of J. S. Phipps, Esq., Palm Beach." *Architectural Forum 38*, no. 5 (May 1923): 49–53.

"Houses of Dr. W. S. Kingsley and Addison Mizner." *Architectural Forum 41* (August 1924): plates 25–28.

"Lake Worth at Twilight." *The Touchstone* (October 1918).

Major, Howard. "A Theory Relating to Spanish and Italian Houses in Florida." *Architectural Forum 45* (August 1926): 97–104.

Price, Matlack. "Latin Architecture in the Playgrounds of the South." *Arts & Decoration 22*, no. 3 (January 1925): La Fontana (Mesker) plates 31–35; El Mirasol (Stotesbury) plates 38–40.

———. "Mediterranean Architecture in Florida." *Architectural Forum 44* (January 1926): 33–40.

Roberts, Mary Fanton. "Back to Health." *The Touchstone 3*, no. 2 (May 1918): 178–81. https://www.google.com/books/edition/The_Touchstone/.

———. "Exotic Beauty of Palm Beach Homes." *Arts & Decoration 20* (December 1923): 22–25.

———. "Palm Beach as a Fountain of Youth and Health." *The Touchstone 3* (April–September 1918): 494–503, Plates 494–500.

Singer, Paris. "Our War Work." *The Touchstone 3*, no. 5 (August 1918): 371–380.

———. "Our War Work." *The Touchstone 3*, no. 7 (October 1918): 52–55.

"Spanish Influence at Florida." *Architectural Forum 41* (August 1924): 73–76. Whitney Publications.

Archives and Collections

Addison Mizner Collection, Historical Society of Palm Beach County.

Addison Mizner Collection & Library, King Library, The Society of The Four Arts.

Boca Raton Historical Society.

NOTES

ACKNOWLEDGMENTS

1. Mary Fanton Roberts, "Exotic Beauty of Palm Beach Homes," *Arts & Decoration 20*, no. 2 (December 1923): 22–25.

FOREWORD

1. "Capt. J. R. DeLamar Leaves $32,282,927," *New York Herald*, May 15, 1920, https://nyshistoricnewspapers.org/.
2. Matlack Price, "Mediterranean Architecture in Florida," *Architectural Forum 44*, no. 1 (January 1926): 33–40.
3. "Palm Beach Society," *Palm Beach Post*, December 13, 1924, https://palmbeachpost.newspapers.com/image/133390604/
4. "The Book Nook." *Palm Beach Post*, February 12, 1933.

ALICE DELAMAR—REMEMBERING ADDISON

1. Kim Mizner Hollins (1932–1992). Ysabel's son, Kim Hollins, was Addison Mizner's godson. In 1970, he established the Fitzgerald and Hollins Custom Woodworking Company in Ft. Lauderdale.
2. Wilson Mizner, a playwright and screenwriter, was Addison Mizner's younger brother. Florence Atkinson, a film actress, was described in Wilson Mizner's will as "a close woman friend" but not his wife.
3. Horace Chase Jr. In 1919, Chase moved to Palm Beach and managed Mizner Industries for his uncle Addison Mizner. An aviation enthusiast, he died in a plane crash in 1928.
4. El Solano, 720 South Ocean Boulevard. Built during the summer of 1919, Mizner sold the house to Harold S. Vanderbilt.
5. In 1923, Horace Chase Jr. developed the Manana Estates subdivision in Palm Beach's North End. Mizner and Marion Sims Wyeth served on Chase's architectural advisory committee.
6. DeLamar bought a four-acre ocean-to-lake parcel from Addison Mizner located at 1425 South Ocean Boulevard. She sold the property's north two hundred feet to Louis Bader, who built Las Puertas Viegas, designed by Marion Sims Wyeth, in 1926. Once she de-landmarked her property during the 1980s and her property was subdivided, her oceanfront house was demolished.
7. Papa Chase was Horace Blanchard Chase Sr., who was married to Addison Mizner's sister Mary Ysabel "Minnie" Mizner (1860–1923). Horace and Minnie operated the Stag's Leap Winery in Napa Valley from 1893 until 1913. Their two children were Ysabel and Horace Jr.

8. Anita Loos. A popular actress and accomplished screenwriter, author of *Gentlemen Prefer Blondes*, Loos was a longtime friend of Wilson Mizner's.

9. Mrs. Stotesbury. The socially prominent Eva Roberts Cromwell Stotesbury was the second Mrs. Edward Stotesbury and Addison Mizner's first residential commission at Palm Beach.

10. Paris Singer's calling card identified him as an Architect-Engineer. Mary Fanton Roberts Papers, Archives of American Art, Smithsonian Institution, Washington, DC. https://www.aaa.si.edu/collections/mary-fanton-roberts-papers-8457.

11. Paris Singer's sons Cecil Singer and George Singer were actively involved in the operation of the Everglades Club.

12. Paris Singer died on June 23, 1932, at a London hotel.

13. In December 1932, following his father's death, Cecil Singer was named president of the Everglades Club.

14. Addison Mizner died in 1933, the year after Paris Singer's death.

15. Marie Dressler. An early silent film actress, she was best known for her comedic talents. A friend to Addison and Wilson, Dressler helped promote the Mizner Development Company's Boca Raton project.

16. Mrs. Henry (Edith Oliver) Rea owned Lagomar. Located at 1560 South Ocean Boulevard, the house was originally designed in 1924 for John Magee.

CHAPTER 1

1. Miss Alva refers to Mrs. Oliver Hazard Perry Belmont, a longtime friend and client of Mizner's. The mother of Consuelo and Harold Vanderbilt, she had divorced William Kissam Vanderbilt in 1896 and married banker Oliver Hazard Perry Belmont, who died in 1908. Alva Belmont lived on Long Island, near Mizner's Port Washington home.

2. The Mizner house, known as the historic Baxter Homestead, was renamed Chateau Myscene, located in Port Washington, New York.

3. Ella Watson Mizner (1836–1915), "Mama Mizner."

4. Florence Sheedy, heir to a Colorado mining fortune, married Isaiah Townsend Burden Jr., whose socially prominent New York family owned the Burden Iron Works.

5. Alex Colebrooke was titled as Lady Alexandra Colebrooke, a lady-in-waiting to Queen Alexandra.

6. Syrie Bernardo Wellcome married playwright Somerset Maugham in June 1917 in a ceremony witnessed by Alex Colebrooke. Syrie had divorced Henry Wellcome, English chemist and cofounder of Wellcome, Burroughs, & Company, who named the playwright as a co-respondent in the divorce case.

7. Isaac Merritt Singer (1811–1875). Born in New York, Singer lived in Paris and in Paignton located in Southwest England. Isaac Singer's

sewing machine was the first to be manufactured with an automatic stitch mechanism, an automatic cloth-feeding device, and an automatically driven needle.

8. Belle was the mother of Daisy Fellowes, a prominent 1930s fashion icon who became the Paris editor of *Harper's Bazaar* magazine.

9. Cecilia "Lily" Henrietta Augusta Graham and Paris Singer were married from 1886 until 1918.

10. Paris Singer became a naturalized American citizen in 1916.

11. Patrick Augustus Singer (1910–1913) was Paris Singer's son from his relationship with Isadora Duncan.

12. Having divorced his first wife, actress Sarah White Ford, in 1913, Augustin Duncan married Margherita Sargent.

13. Bellevue was the former Paillard Palace Hotel that Singer first planned as the site for his medical research institute. When opposition to his plan developed, he permitted Isadora Duncan to use it as a school and living quarters for her adopted daughters and dance pupils. In 1914, it was converted into a military hospital.

14. Elsa Maxwell was an author, screenwriter, newspaper columnist, and party hostess who became café society's leading press agent during the 1920s and 1930s.

CHAPTER 2

1. Gus Jordahn, a former lifeguard, was the owner of Gus' Bath, the oceanfront bath house with saltwater swimming pools located on Worth Avenue. Paris Singer bought the facility in 1925, converting one of the pools into the private Palm Beach Swimming Club for members of the Everglades Club.

2. Dr. Sherman Downs of Saratoga Springs was the physician for The Breakers and Royal Poinciana hotels who also became the Everglades Club's resident doctor.

CHAPTER 3

1. La Billucia, Bill and Lucy Kingsley's Mizner-designed house, was located at 1200 South Ocean Boulevard.

2. "Mr. Paris Singer Divorced," *Birmingham Daily Post*, December 1, 1918 (England). Separated since 1910, according to court testimony by witnesses, Paris Singer and Joan Bates had been living together since 1914, having begun a relationship in 1912.

3. During the last weekend of March 1918, Paris Singer and Addison Mizner motored to Miami, where they spent the weekend visiting Vizcaya, the James Deering estate. Upon their return, Singer mentioned in several interviews that the architecture for his Palm Beach project would be built to look as if it had always been there, like Vizcaya.

4. At the time, the Everglades began west of Parker Avenue in West Palm Beach.

5. El Solano, 720 South Ocean Boulevard.

6. Alligator Joe's alligator pens were located at the end of the Jungle Trail between the mainland and Lone Cabbage Island, believed to be near where a bridge to Everglades Island was eventually built.

7. During the summer and fall of 1918, Paris Singer leased West Palm Beach's Novelty Works owned by the Dade Lumber Company to supply roof and floor tiles for his Everglades Club project. Upon completion of the club, Singer organized the Los Manos Pottery & Tuileries on South Dixie Highway, West Palm Beach. The facility was named for the site of Parisian tile factories that later became the site for the Jardin des Tuileries. The following year, Singer sold the plant to Addison Mizner. Renamed Las Manos Potteries, Mizner hired his nephew Horace Chase Jr. to manage the workshop complex on Bunker Road.

8. Handwritten note by Alice DeLamar at end of the text: "November 11, 1918. A convalescent home would not be needed. The new edifice would open as a club."

CHAPTER 4

1. Bula Edmondson Croker, a prominent Native American educator and suffragette, was born on the Cherokee Nation's tribal land in Oklahoma.

2. Noted Palm Beach philanthropist John C. King (1864–1936) was a Chicago stock and bond broker. Mrs. King was a niece of Marshall Field.

3. During the first several years, the lakefront terrace was known as the Venetian Landing before it was renamed the Orange Gardens.

4. Sportsman Craig Biddle (1879–1947) was a competitive national and international tennis player, winning the Florida Cup in 1917. San Francisco-born Virginia Graham Fair "Birdie" Vanderbilt was a longtime friend of Mizner's, as was her sister Tessie Fair Oelrichs. In 1899, Birdie married William Kissam Vanderbilt II. The couple separated in 1909 but did not divorce until 1927.

5. The Stotesburys' El Mirasol was named for and initially modeled on designer Albert Herter's family estate named El Mirasol, designed by Delano and Aldrich in 1909, located in Santa Barbara. Albert Herter and his wife, artist Adele Herter, worked on the first plans for El Mirasol at Palm Beach before Mizner arrived.

6. Financier E. Clarence Jones (1868–1926) was a Wall Street stockbroker who headed the E. Clarence Jones & Company banking house. Jones's Villa Yalta was located at the northeast corner of North County Road and Sunrise Avenue. It was later converted into The Patio night club, adjacent to the Paramount Theatre.

7. Built side by side on parcels acquired from John S. Phipps, Gurnee and Marie Louise Wanamaker Munn's house Louwana and Charles and Mary Astor Paul Munn's Amado were built when Ocean Boulevard ran east of their houses.

8. Mary Adelaide Yerkes, the widow of wealthy industrialist Charles Tyson Yerkes, was briefly married in 1906 to Addison's brother Wilson Mizner, resulting in weeks of newspaper headlines.

CHAPTER 5

1. 720 South Ocean Boulevard.

2. The house was named for Solano County, where the Mizner family's California home was in the town of Benicia. Also possible, *solano* is the Spanish word for "east wind."

3. Mizner's sister Mary Ysabel "Minnie" Mizner was married to Horace Blanchard Chase Sr. Her son was Horace Jr.

4. Stag's Leap Winery, Napa Valley, California.

5. "Home in Palm Beach Is Invaded and Searched by Dry Law Officers," *Palm Beach Post*, September 22, 1920. Haig & Haig, Royal Scotch, and other expensive brands from Ireland and England, described as enough to "fill five fish barrels," was found locked in the cellar of Amado, the Charles Munn residence.

6. Bobby Neuman was one of Addison Mizner's draftsmen.

CHAPTER 6

1. Harold S. Vanderbilt, known to friends as Mike, bought Mizner's house El Solano located at 720 South Ocean Boulevard.

2. E. W. Histed was a famous society portrait photographer whose lakeside Jungle Studio was located on an ocean-to-lake parcel on the north side of Royal Palm Way. Mizner rented a house from Histed on County Road that was later sold to Bessemer Properties, which developed it as part of Phipps Plaza.

3. Mizner hosted popular parties at the house that he called "The Shack."

4. 1921. The John S. Phipps house on North County Road was named Casa Bendita, likened to a Spanish castle. That year, Mizner designed 450 Worth Avenue for Leonard Thomas, 121 El Bravo Way, for Charles J. Winn; for himself, he began building Concha Marina at 102 Jungle Road.

5. Cooper C. Lightbown was elected mayor of Palm Beach in 1922. Lightbown was also the first to suggest and implement standards for the town of Palm Beach building codes and permits.

6. George Jonas was a co-developer of Royal Park who also platted and developed Ocean Vista subdivision on South Ocean Boulevard, south of the Bingham property.

7. In December 1918, Cecilia "Lilly" Henrietta Augusta Singer divorced her husband, Paris Singer, in London on grounds of desertion and misconduct, ending their thirty-year marriage. Court documents show that Singer separated from his wife in 1910, upon the birth of his son Patrick with Isadora Duncan. He began a relationship with Joan Bates in 1912–1913 and had lived with her since 1914 in England, France, and the United States. A year after the divorce, Singer and Bates married in New York.

8. Politician, publisher, and financier Joseph Earman was a partner in the firm publishing the *Palm Beach Daily News* and *Palm Beach Post*. Earman sold his interest in the *Palm Beach Post* to his partner, D. H. Conkling, in January 1921.

9. February 1923.

10. Standard Oil Trust scion William Gray Warden and his wife, Agnes Morgan Warden.

CHAPTER 7

1. Concha Marina, 102 Jungle Road. Isabel Dodge Sloane, daughter of Detroit automotive manufacturer John F. Dodge, was briefly married to George Sloane.

2. 1800 South Ocean Boulevard, demolished in 2021, was known as Sin Cuidado.

3. Mizner built a bridge across the alley connecting the four-story apartment with the office. Alice DeLamar recalled, "He used to say, 'No one will want to buy this place from under me.'" The top floor had a magnificent view, as did the library studio. There was a terrace for his animals. The monkey, Johnny Mizner, also possibly known as Johnnie Brown, is believed to be buried in the patio behind the tower apartment with an inscribed gravestone.

4. Later, when Mizner Alley was completed, Mr. Wead was dressed in white with a red fez on his head and a red sash around his enormous girth. It became his duty to stand with a large red umbrella at the entrance to the Alley and act as doorman for cars that drove by, always with his wide smile as greeting.

5. Mizner's clients were Florence and Isaiah Townsend Burden Jr. While Mr. Burden's silk-stocking family enjoyed Social Register status, his wife, the former Florence Sheedy, inherited one of Colorado's largest banking, mining, and cattle fortunes. Her sister Marie married Robert L. Livingston, a member of one of New York's oldest Knickerbocker families.

6. Oil magnate Joshua Cosden and his second wife, Eleanor "Nell" Neves Cosden.

7. In 1923, the Cosdens bought an ocean-to-lake parcel on the north side of the Palm Beach Country Club. After Hugh and Anna Dodge

Dillman acquired the Cosdens' house in 1925, they renamed it Playa Riente.

8. Mizner set sail for Europe aboard the RMS *Mauretania* on May 29, 1923.

9. Pennsylvania railroad heiress Peggy Thayer accompanied Mizner and Nell Cosden on their European buying trip.

10. Alex Waugh, formerly associated with Partridges in London, was an antique furniture expert, not the British novelist who spelled his name Alec Waugh.

11. Mizner attended the University of Salamanca.

12. Burton Holmes was the Gilded Age's most celebrated travel expert and lecturer.

13. President of the Emerson Drug Company, Isaac Edward Emerson manufactured patent medicine cure-alls, making his first fortune as the "Bromo-Seltzer King." His daughter Margaret married Alfred Gwynne Vanderbilt.

14. Alexander Pollock Moore was the American ambassador to Spain from 1923 until 1925.

15. A former New York State assemblyman and state senator, Jimmy Walker served as New York City's mayor from 1926 until 1932.

16. Lillian Russell (1861–1922). A famous American actress and singer whose fourth husband was Alexander Moore.

17. Artists Achille Angeli and Frederico Angeli re-created the Davanzati murals for the Joshua Cosdens' villa at Palm Beach. The Angeli brothers also did murals for Alice DeLamar's house on South Ocean Boulevard and the Armada Dining Room at the Everglades Club.

CHAPTER 8

1. *The Many Mizners* was the title of the first volume of Mizner's autobiography, published in 1932, that referred to his brothers and sister.

2. Paris Singer suffered from insomnia.

3. For the Cosdens' Palm Beach villa, Sert designed eight twenty-foot-high, decorative panels depicting "The Great Adventure of Sinbad the Sailor." Painted in black and silver with tromp l'oeil red velvet curtains against a background of solid gold camaieu, they were exhibited in February 1924 at New York's Wildenstein Galleries before installation at Palm Beach.

4. Via Mizner's first tenants began occupying their apartments and storefronts in December 1924.

5. Porte Quinn was a real estate broker and investor associated with Singer and Mizner.

6. Artist and book illustrator Victor Searles was the nephew of interior decorator Edward Frank Searles, who had inherited his wife's more than

$30-million fortune when she died in 1891. Following his uncle's death in 1920, and after a publicized will contest, Victor Searles was awarded $4.5 million from his uncle's estate.

CHAPTER 9

1. In March 1889, Mizner's father, Lansing Bond Mizner, was appointed by President Benjamin Harrison as the envoy extraordinary and minister plenipotentiary to Central America, headquartered in Guatemala City.
2. Ray Goetz was a composer and theatrical manager associated with Irving Berlin and husband of actress Irene Bordoni.
3. United States Senator William Borah.

CHAPTER 10

1. Dr. William Garrison Mizner died in 1926, survived by his wife, Frances T. Mizner, as well as brothers Addison and Wilson.
2. William "Bill" Willard Crocker, president of the Crocker National Bank, and his wife, Ruth Hobart Crocker.
3. Samuel F. B. Morse, president of the Del Monte Property Company, was the builder of the Lodge at Pebble Beach. Beginning in 1916, Morse developed most of the Monterey Peninsula into an eighteen-thousand-acre recreational resort and exclusive residential area.
4. A former oil company executive, Harry Hunt, and his wife, Jane Selby Hunt, owned the five thousand-acre El Sur Ranch.
5. Harry and Jane Hunt's Spanish Colonial home designed by Clarence Tantau was featured in *Arts & Decoration 23*, no. 4 (August 1925).
6. Marion Hollins's brother McKim Hollins married Ysabel Chase at Pebble Beach in 1930.

CHAPTER 11

1. Madame Frances Alda (1879–1952), an operatic soprano, born Fanny Jane Davis in New Zealand, who frequently sang with Enrico Caruso at the Metropolitan Opera.
2. Paris Singer also hosted famous string quartets, playing often in the late afternoon in the large living room of his Chinese Villa on Peruvian Avenue.
3. Mary Garden (1874–1967) was a famous operatic soprano, known as the "Sarah Bernhardt of opera."
4. Louise Beatty Homer (1871–1947) was a renowned operatic contralto. The Seligmans, known as the "American Rothschilds," were Henry and Addie Walter Seligman, longtime Palm Beach residents who were members of the Everglades Club and the Bath & Tennis Club.

5. Stage and silent screen actress Fannie Ward (1872–1952) became a member of the Sun & Surf Club during the 1930s.

AFTERWORD

1. Letter, April 19, 1926, Paris Singer to Addison Mizner. Mizner Library Foundation Collection.
2. Donald Curl, *Florida Architecture of Addison Mizner* (New York: Dover Publications, 1992).

MIZNER INDUSTRIES

1. "Palatial Residence for L. T. Highleyman on New Palm Island," *Miami Daily Metropolis*, July 16, 1920.
2. Donald Curl, *Mizner's Florida: American Resort Architecture* (New York: Architectural History Foundation and MIT Press, 1984).

INDEX

Page references for figures are italicized.